刘谦功 主编

刘谦功 舒燕 于洁 编著

文化欣赏读本 〈上〉
汉英对照

Exploring Chinese Culture
A CHINESE READER *I*

北京语言大学出版社
BEIJING LANGUAGE AND CULTURE
UNIVERSITY PRESS

中央广播电视大学音像出版社
MULTIMEDIA PRESS, OPEN UNIVERSITY OF CHINA

U0618759

图书在版编目(CIP)数据

中国文化欣赏读本.上:汉英对照 / 刘谦功主编.
-- 北京:北京语言大学出版社,2014.1(2022.10 重印)

ISBN 978-7-5619-3678-8

Ⅰ.①中… Ⅱ.①刘… Ⅲ.①汉语 – 对外汉语教学–
语言读物 ②中华文化 – 基本知识 – 汉语、英语 Ⅳ.①H195.5
②K203

中国版本图书馆CIP数据核字(2014)第015778号

书　　名	中国文化欣赏读本. 上. 汉英对照
	ZHONGGUO WENHUA XINSHANG DUBEN. SHANG. HAN YING DUIZHAO
中文编辑	李佳琳
英文翻译	罗正鹏　孙齐圣
英文审订	【美】Andrew Bauer
英文编辑	辛　颖
版式设计	北京彩奇风企业管理策划有限公司
责任印制	邝　天
出版发行	北京语言大学出版社
社　　址	北京市海淀区学院路15号　邮政编码:100083
网　　址	www.blcup.com
电　　话	编辑部 8610-8230 1016
	发行部 8610-8230 3650/3591/3648
	读者服务部 8610-8230 3653/3908
网上订购	8610-8230 3668(国内)　service@blcup.com
印　　刷	天津嘉恒印务有限公司
经　　销	全国新华书店
版　　次	2014年1月第1版　2022年10月第6次印刷
开　　本	787mm×1092mm　1/16　印张:8
字　　数	167千字
书　　号	ISBN 978-7-5619-3678-8 / H·13266
定　　价	78.00元

凡有印装质量问题,本社负责调换。电话:8610-82303590
Printed in China

前　言

　　《中国文化欣赏读本》与《中国文化欣赏》DVD 配套，力图从多个角度生动鲜活地展示中国丰富多彩的文化。本书既可以作为面向中外各界人士的读物，也可以作为汉语学习者的教材。

　　在内容上，本书选取的文化主题来源于美国汉语教学第一线，是在密西根州立大学孔子学院的调研结果的基础上确定的，既涵盖了当地汉语教材中的文化点，也尽可能地照顾到了外国人对中国文化的兴趣点。

　　在编排上，本书每一个文化主题由四个小板块组成，即"导入"、"正文"、"三言两语"、"小链接"。"导入"试图通过各种人物、事件或场景使读者轻松愉快地进入主题，"正文"是对每一主题较为全面、深入的介绍，"三言两语"是中外各界人士对相应主题的评价或感受，"小链接"旨在拓展与主题相关的知识面。需要说明的是，为了让读者看到一些真实材料，我们没有修改"三言两语"中外国朋友们汉语说得不太准确的地方。

　　本书图文并茂，尽可能使中国文化直观可感，且全书所有内容均为中英文对照，使读者可以通过双语来很好地理解所有内容。

　　《中国文化欣赏读本》既可与《中国文化欣赏》DVD 配套使用，也可单独使用，因为本书与 DVD 虽然所选主题相同，但都自成体系，二者之间既有内在的联系，分开使用也不影响各自的完整性。作为编者，我们真诚地希望本书能对外国朋友理解与欣赏中国文化有所裨益。

编者

2013 年 11 月

FOREWORD

Exploring Chinese Culture, A Chinese Reader is a supplementary book to the DVD version of *Exploring Chinese Culture*. This book, a vivid presentation of the rich and colorful Chinese culture, can not only be used as reading material for domestic and foreign readers of different walks of life, but can also serve as textbook for learners of Chinese.

The cultural themes in this book are selected from the forefront of Chinese teaching in America following the survey conducted by the Confucius Institute at Michigan State University. It not only contains the cultural elements of Chinese textbooks in Michigan, but also fully considers foreigner interest regarding Chinese culture.

The cultural themes in this book comprise four sections, "Introduction", "Text", "A Few Remarks" and "Additional Information". The "Introduction" section initiates readers into the topic by presenting various characters, events or backgrounds; the "Text" is a comprehensive and in-depth description of the theme; "A Few Remarks" contains the comments or feedback provided by people from different walks of life, both in China and abroad; "Additional Information" is designed as an extension of knowledge related to the theme. It should be noted that we didn't revise the non-native Chinese produced by some foreigners so as to present readers with real language materials.

The articles are accompanied by excellent illustrations helpful for a direct and vivid experience of Chinese culture. In addition, the bilingual (English and Chinese) contents of this book assist for a more rapid and better understanding of the cultural themes.

Exploring Chinese Culture, A Chinese Reader can either be used together with the DVD version of *Exploring Chinese Culture*, or used independently. Though the book has the same cultural themes with the DVD, they in fact possess independent systems, thus they can be used separately without losing their completeness. As the compilers of this book, we sincerely hope it can prove beneficial to foreigner understanding of Chinese culture.

The Compilers

November, 2013

目录 CONTENTS

传统节日　Traditional Festivals

002　春节 ｜ The Spring Festival

007　元宵节 ｜ The Lantern Festival

012　中秋节 ｜ The Mid-Autumn Festival

传统习俗　Traditional Customs

018　生日习俗 ｜ Birthday Conventions

023　生肖动物 ｜ Zodiac Animals

028　中国龙 ｜ Chinese Dragon

中国艺术　Chinese Arts

034　京剧 ｜ Beijing Opera

040　园林 ｜ Chinese Gardens

文化符号　Chinese Culture Symbols

048　文房四宝 ｜ Four Treasures of Study

053　汉字 ｜ Chinese Characters

🔅 名胜古迹　Tourism Highlights

060 兵马俑 ｜ Terracotta Warriors

066 平遥古城 ｜ Pingyao Ancient City

072 布达拉宫 ｜ The Potala Palace

🔅 生活在中国 Living in China

080 餐桌礼仪 ｜ Dinner Etiquette

085 茶文化 ｜ Tea Culture

090 中国服饰 ｜ Chinese Style Clothing

🔅 民间工艺　Folk Arts

096 剪纸 ｜ Paper Cutting

101 景泰蓝 ｜ Chinese Cloisonné

🔅 民间运动　Folk Sports

108 空竹 ｜ Chinese Yo-Yo

113 武术—拳术 ｜ Martial Arts–Chinese Boxing

Traditional Festivals

传统節日

春 节
The Spring Festival

春节俗称"过年"。传说古时候有一个叫作"年"的怪兽，每到腊月三十晚上就出来吃人。后来人们发现"年"怕红、怕火、怕响，于是就在腊月三十这天在大门贴上红色的福字和春联，在院子里燃放噼啪作响的爆竹，以便把"年"赶跑。作为中国的农历新年，春节也是全世界华人共同庆祝的节日。

The Spring Festival is commonly known as *guo nian* in Chinese. There is a legend that in ancient times, a monster called *nian* went out to eat people every December 30th (lunar calendar) in the evening. Later, after finding that *nian* was afraid of the color red, fire as well as loud noise, people put up a red Chinese character *fu* (fortune) and Spring Festival couplets on their doors as well as let off firecrackers with crackling sound in their yards in order to discharge *nian*. As the beginning of a new year in Chinese lunar calendar, the Spring Festival is also celebrated by Chinese people worldwide.

在漫长的历史发展过程中，过春节时一些具有原始信仰色彩的习俗逐渐消失，而富有生活情趣和积极意义的习俗则被保留下来。

春节的准备工作一般从腊月二十三日就开始了，主要是扫尘（即打扫房屋）和贴门神、春联、年画、窗花等。春联是对联的一种，因为在春节时张贴而被称作"春联"，

During the long history of the Spring Festival, some customs related to primitive belief gradually disappeared while some others possessing life interest and positive meaning remain.

The preparation for the Spring Festival, which generally begins from December 23rd (lunar calendar), includes cleaning the house, pasting pictures of the Door-God, Spring Festival couplets, New Year pictures, paper-cuts for window decoration and so on. As a kind

内容大多是与新春有关的吉祥祝语。年画是中国民间传统艺术，汉代（前206—公元220）已在民间广泛流传，宋代（960—1279）开始出现木版年画并有了年画作坊，清代（1616—1911）大盛，最著名的是天津杨柳青年画、苏州桃花坞年画、山东潍县年画。

杨柳青年画，刘谦功摄

Yangliuqing New Year picture, photographed by Liu Qiangong

农历十二月的最后一天是除夕，又叫"年三十"。这天晚上人们通宵不睡，一家人围坐在一起宴饮谈笑，尽情欢乐，以迎接新年的到来，这就是"守岁"。除夕晚上的饭菜非常丰盛，俗称"年夜饭"。北方人大多吃饺子，因饺子与"交子①"谐音，寓意辞旧迎新，富裕吉祥；南方人大多吃年糕，因年糕与"年年高"谐音，象征生活一年比一年美好。无论南方、北方过年都要吃鱼，取"年年有余"之意。这些习俗表达了人们对幸福生活的祈盼。

of antithetical couplets, the Spring Festival couplets, mostly being blessings for good luck in the new year, get their name because they are put up during the Spring Festival. The Spring Festival pictures, a traditional Chinese folk art, have been spread widely since the Han Dynasty (206 BC-AD 220). In the Song Dynasty (960-1279), wood engraving pictures and workshops appeared. New Year pictures enjoyed great popularity in the Qing Dynasty (1616-1911). Among them, the most well-known are Yangliuqing New Year pictures in Tianjin City, Taohuawu New Year pictures in Suzhou City and Weixian New Year pictures in Shandong Province.

The last day of December in the lunar calendar is the eve of the lunar New Year, which is also called *nian sanshi* in Chinese when the whole family stays up all night and sits around, eating, chatting and laughing in great joy to greet the New Year, which is known as *shou sui*. The rich meal of that night is named as *nianyefan* in Chinese. Most Northern Chinese eat dumplings with the implied meaning of ringing out the Old Year and ringing in the New Year in wealth and good fortune. The pronunciation of dumpling in Chinese is *jiaozi*, similar to another Chinese word *jiaozi* [1] ; Southern Chinese however mostly eat New Year cakes whose Chinese name *niangao* is similar to *niannian gao*, symbolizing that life gets better and better year after year. Moreover, both Northern and Southern Chinese eat fish, hoping for *niannian you yu*, which means enjoying prosperity every year because *yu*, "fish" in Chinese, can also

---

① 交子："子"即"子时"，是中国传统的"十二时辰"中的第一个时辰，即当代时间的晚23点至凌晨1点。在除夕之夜的这个时间段，旧的一年结束，新的一年开始，故称"交子"。

① *Jiaozi*: zi, also called *zishi*, refers to the the period of the day from 11 pm to 1 am. This period of time on the lunar New Year's Eve is referred to as *jiaozi* when the old year ends and the new year begins.

拜年是春节必不可少的活动。每逢新春佳节人们都要走亲访友，互致新年问候。20 世纪末，随着电脑和手机的普及，通过电子邮件或短信拜年成为一种时尚。

除上述习俗外，中国人过春节时还有不少娱乐活动，如放鞭炮、舞龙、舞狮、逛庙会等。

舞龙
The dragon dance

庙会是中国民间传统集市贸易的一种形式，指在寺庙内或附近地区定期举办的集市。中国各地庙会很多，可说是形形色色。近年来不少地区为了开发当地经济和文化资源，相继恢复和举办了一些影响较大的庙会，如北京的地坛庙会、上海的城隍庙会等，取得了很好的经济效益和社会效益。

随着社会生活的发展，中国人的春节习俗也在发生变化，例如除夕之夜到饭店吃年夜饭，春节期间外出旅行，围炉守岁被观看中央电视台春节联欢晚会所取代。然而传统文化的精

be interpreted as "abundance". All of these customs reveal people's hope and prayer for a happy life.

Paying New Year calls is also essential. During the Spring Festival, people always visit relatives and friends and exchange New Year greetings. At the end of the 20th century, the popularity of computers and mobile phones has made it fashionable to send New Year greetings via email or short messages.

Apart from the above-mentioned customs, Chinese people also have many other recreational activities during the Spring Festival such as setting off firecrackers, the dragon dance, the lion dance, and going to the temple fair.

The temple fair is a form of traditional Chinese folk fair trade, referring to the fair held regularly within or near the temple. All sorts of temple fairs are seen all around China. In recent years, a number of influential temple fairs in many regions, such as Beijing Ditan Temple Fair and Shanghai City God Temple Fair, have been restored and organized in order to develop local economic and cultural resources, achieving good economic and social benefits.

With the development of social life, Chinese customs during the Spring Festival are also undergoing some changes such as eating in restaurants, going out for travel during the festival, and watching CCTV Spring Festival Gala instead of staying up late surrounding the stove on New Year's Eve. The essence of traditional culture, however, has not changed. For example, "filial piety" is still so stressed that people will not only give gift money to children

北京地坛春节庙会，刘谦功摄　　*Beijing Ditan Spring Festival Temple Fair, photographed by Liu Qiangong*

髓并没有变，例如讲求"孝道"。为了祝福长辈健康长寿，过年时人们在给孩子压岁钱的同时，也不会忘记给老人红包。

　　春节一方面体现了中国人重伦理、重亲情的文化传统，另一方面也在不断融入新的生活内容，以满足当代人物质与精神文化的需求。

but also red packets to elderly people during the Spring Festival to express wishes of good health and longevity for the elders.

On the one hand, the Spring Festival reflects the Chinese cultural tradition of valuing ethics and family affection. On the other hand, it has also constantly absorbed new contents of life to meet contemporary people's needs for material and spiritual culture.

三言两语 A FEW REMARKS

　　新年，特别是春节，是一年中童心最感欢乐的时候。现在回想起来，那些庆祝节日的鞭炮声、锣鼓声，那些穿街过巷的狮子舞队，那些老少相逢的互相祝福，那些吐着芳香的花卉摆设……种种声响、形象和气氛，都像银幕上所显示的一一涌现眼前。它使我进入一种异乎日常的神异境界。

　　[中国] 钟敬文，男，民俗学家

The New Year, especially the Spring Festival, is the happiest time for children.
In retrospect, all sounds, images and atmospheres—the firecrackers, the beating of gongs and drums to celebrate the festival, the lion dance teams going through the streets, the blessings between old and young people and the floral display in fragrance—emerge before my eyes as if they were on the silver screen. They led me into an extraordinary and miraculous realm.

[China] Zhong Jingwen, male, folklorist

一提春节，就会想到团圆饭、守岁、红包、舞狮、鞭炮等等。春节是全家团圆的日子，在外地工作的游子都渴望在春节回老家与家人相聚。我对春节最深刻的印象是映入眼帘的尽是一片红彤彤，以及奶奶所坚持的禁忌，如春节期间不可说不吉利的话、不可扫地，摔破东西就得赶紧说"岁岁平安"，等等。

[马来西亚] 覃宝仪，女，研究生

When mentioning the Spring Festival in conversation, people will always think of the reunion dinners, staying up late on New Year's Eve, the red packets, the lion dance, firecrackers and so on. All people working in places far away from home look forward to returning home for family reunion during the Spring Festival, a period of time when the whole family gets together. My deepest impression of the Spring Festival is that everything in sight is red and that my grandma insists on avoiding some taboos. For example, saying unlucky words and sweeping the floor are not allowed during the festival. If you break something, you need to say *suisui ping'an* (everlasting peace year after year) quickly. (*sui* can mean either "break" or "year" in Chinese)

[Malaysia] Qin Baoyi, female, graduate student

小链接 ADDITIONAL INFORMATION

为庆祝春节，中国中央电视台从 1983 年起每年除夕都要举办大型综艺性文艺晚会，即"春节联欢晚会"，简称"春晚"。目前看春晚已成为当代中国人过年的新民俗、新文化。春晚在演出规模和演员阵容、播出时长和海内外观众收视率方面创下世界综艺晚会三项世界之最，入选中国世界纪录协会世界收视率最高的综艺晚会、世界上播出时间最长的综艺晚会、世界上演员最多的综艺晚会。

中央电视台春节联欢晚会场景
A scene from the CCTV Spring Festival Gala

To celebrate the Spring Festival, CCTV holds the Spring Festival Gala, a large variety show called *chunwan* in short, on every Chinese New Year's Eve since 1983. Watching the gala has become a new custom and culture for contemporary Chinese people to celebrate the festival. The gala ranks first among world evening variety shows in terms of performance scale, cast, broadcast time and audience rating home and abroad. It is also selected as the evening gala with the highest audience rating, the longest broadcast time, and largest number of performers according to the China World Records Association.

元宵节
The Lantern Festival

元宵节，又称"灯节"。这个节日，由灯而生而精彩。1982年，在哈尔滨举办的冰灯活动被正式定名为"冰灯节"，时间一般是1月上旬至2月中旬。哈尔滨冰灯将北方特有的天然冰雪与现代灯光及声控技术巧妙结合在一起，通过堆塑、雕刻、造型、置景等方法营造了一个童话般的冰雪世界，为当代元宵节增添了新的色彩。

Yuanxiao Festival, also called the Lantern Festival, is quite splendid because of the lanterns. In 1982, the ice lantern show in Harbin was officially named as the Ice Lantern Festival which is generally held from the beginning of January to mid-February. Through ingeniously combining the natural ice and snow peculiar to Northern China with modern lighting and voice technology, Harbin ice lanterns create a fairy land of ice and snow by means of decoration, carving, modeling and set construction, adding a new color to the contemporary Lantern Festival.

哈尔滨冰灯
Harbin ice lanterns

元宵节是农历正月十五，"元"有"开端"的意思，"宵"代表"夜晚"，因为这天晚上是一年中的第一个月圆之夜，所以被称为"元宵"。一般认为元宵节始于汉代（前206—公元220），随着佛教的传入出现了正月十五之夜在宫廷和寺院里燃灯的习俗,后来这一习俗由宫廷传入民间。

The Yuanxiao Festival falls on January 15th of the lunar calendar. *Yuan* means "beginning" and *xiao* means "evening". It is called *yuanxiao* because it is the first night of each year with a full-moon. It is generally recognized that the Lantern Festival began in the Han Dynasty (206 BC-AD 220) when, after the introduction of Buddhism, the custom of lighting lanterns in palaces and temples appeared and spread

唐代（618—907）元宵节观灯的习俗得到很大发展，宋代（960—1279）出现了灯谜，明代（1368—1644）以后又增加了戏曲表演，使元宵节的活动更加丰富多彩。

元宵节花灯的种类很多，北京就曾以生产宫廷使用的宫灯和纱灯著称，其中用于元宵节的"皇家花灯"由宫中能工巧匠精制而成，皇太后将其赐予文武百官，以示"与民同乐"之意。

花灯
Festival lanterns

元宵节中国各地都会举办灯会，如江苏秦淮灯会、四川自贡灯会、广东佛山灯会、福建泉州灯会、河南洛阳灯会等。20世纪80年代以来，中国一些城市还出现了不少新型灯会，如哈尔滨冰灯会、北京三里屯国际时尚街区灯会等等。新型灯会体现了中国传统节日与现代生活的融合，成为当代人元宵观灯、休闲和旅游的好去处。

to the whole society. The great development of the custom of viewing lanterns in the Tang Dynasty (618-907) and the appearance of lantern riddles in the Song Dynasty (960-1279) and opera performance in the Ming Dynasty (1368-1644) make the activities of the Lantern Festival all the more rich.

There are a great variety of festival lanterns during the Lantern Festival. Beijing was once known for its production of palace lanterns and gauze lanterns. The royal lantern used in the Lantern Festival is refined by skillful craftsmen in the palace and granted by the empress dowager to civil and military officials possessing the symbolic meaning of "sharing happiness with ordinary people".

During the Lantern Festival, lantern shows are held throughout China such as the Qinhuai Lantern Show in Jiangsu Province, the Zigong Lantern Show in sichuan Province, the Quanzhou Lantern Show in Fujian Province, and the Luoyang Lantern Show in Henan Province. Since the 1980s, some cities have witnessed the appearance of some new lantern shows such as the Harbin Ice Lantern Show and the Beijing Sanlitun International Fashion District Lantern Show, which reflect the integration of Chinese traditional festivals and modern life and offer contemporary people a good place for lantern viewing, recreation and travel.

During the Lantern Festival in ancient China, young girls were allowed to go out freely and play together, and single men and women could meet their lovers. Married women would pray for a happy marriage, continuation of the

江苏秦淮灯会　*Qinhuai Lantern Show in Jiangsu Province*

在中国古代，元宵节也是年轻女孩儿被允许外出自由活动、结伴嬉游及未婚男女与情人相会的日子。已婚妇女则会在这一天祈求婚姻美满、子嗣绵延、身体康健。从传统意义来看，元宵节的风俗从一个侧面表达了妇女们的生活愿望。

元宵节的另一个活动是猜灯谜，灯谜就是贴在或挂在彩灯上的谜语，又叫"灯虎"。因为灯谜内容常常艰深难懂，不易猜中，好像用弓箭射老虎那么难，所以猜灯谜在古代又被称作"射灯虎"。一边赏灯一边猜谜是元宵节的传统活动。由于灯谜能考验人的智慧，所以自宋代产生以来一直受到人们的喜爱。灯谜内容丰富，形式多样，既有知识性，又有趣味性和娱乐性，至今仍是节日游园会上不可缺少的活动。

family line and good health. In a traditional sense, the customs of the festival reveal women's wishes in life from one perspective.

Another activity is guessing lantern riddles which are posted on or hung on the lantern and also known as "lantern tigers". Since guessing the elusive lantern riddles is as hard as to shoot a tiger with bow and arrow, it is also called "shooting a lantern tiger". Enjoying the lanterns while guessing the riddles is a traditional activity in the Lantern Festival. Guessing riddles, which can test people's wisdom, has been popular since the Song Dynasty and remains to be indispensable in festival parties for the riddles are rich in content and form, as well as informative, interesting and entertaining.

A representative food of the Lantern Festival are rice glue balls. It is said that the custom of eating rice glue balls on the lunar day of January 15th also began in the Song Dynasty. Apart from displaying festival lanterns and

猜灯谜
Guessing lantern riddles

元宵节的节日食品是"元宵"。传说正月十五吃元宵的习俗也是从宋代开始的。当时人们过元宵节除了悬挂花灯、燃放烟火以外还要互赠"圆子"（即元宵），以象征在新年的第一个月圆之夜合家欢聚团圆。

元宵节是一个古老的节日，也是一个欢乐的节日。无论从节日时间还是节日习俗的意义来看，元宵节都是春节的有机组成部分。作为春节庆典的压轴活动，元宵节以其热闹、欢庆的气氛，表达了人们对新年幸福生活的美好祝愿。

setting off fireworks, people also give each other *yuanzi* (rice glue balls) as gifts, symbolizing family reunion on the first full-moon night of the new year.

The Lantern Festival is both ancient as well as cheerful. It is an organic component of the Spring Festival when considering either its time or the meaning of its customs. As the finale of the Spring Festival celebration, the lively and joyous Lantern Festival reveals people's best wishes for a happy life in the new year.

元宵节的灯，田琨摄
Lanterns during the Lantern Festival, photographed by Tian Kun

三言两语 A FEW REMARKS

我年轻的时候，在元宵节的第二天，也就是正月十六，要"走百病"。村里的女人们聚在一起，走墙边、过桥头或去郊外，这样可以除病除灾。现在我岁数大了，这多少年都没出去走了，现在的小年轻的也不讲这些了。其实走走也好，多活动活动，身子骨肯定硬朗。

[中国] 池金花，女，农民

When I was young, I would "walk sickness" on the lunar day of January 16th, the day after the Lantern Festival. Women in the village got together to walk along the walls, walk across the bridges or go to the countryside with the purpose of expelling disease and disaster. Since I have become old now, I have not gone out for many years. Presently, young people do not care about this anymore. However, in fact, going for walks will surely make people hale and hearty.

[China] Chi Jinhua, female, peasant

吃元宵、赏花灯、舞狮子是元宵节几项最重要的民间习俗。每逢元宵节，街上人山人海，到处都是节日的气氛，别提多喜兴了。我特别喜欢这种气氛，我觉得这热闹里面有一种特别温馨的东西。

[中国] 张旭，男，公司职员

Eating rice glue balls and enjoying festival lanterns and lion dances are among the most important folk customs of the Lantern Festival. During the festival, there are always seas of people on the streets with a festive and indescribably happy atmosphere everywhere. I love this atmosphere because I discover something warm in the noise and excitement.

[China] Zhang Xu, male, company employee

小链接 ADDITIONAL INFORMATION

泰国也有灯节，叫水灯节，时间是泰历十二月十五日夜晚。传说水灯节始于 13 世纪泰国的第一个王朝——素可泰时期，是从宫廷传入民间的。漂水灯是水灯节的主要活动，来源于祭奠水神的宗教仪式，后来发展成为庆祝丰收、感谢河神及青年男女寻觅如意伴侣、祈求有情人终成眷属的欢乐节日。水灯的样式有莲花、凤凰、佛塔等，千姿百态，美不胜收。人们在放水灯之

放水灯
Floating the water lantern

前会许下一个美好的愿望，让水灯带着这一愿望漂向远方。

Thailand also has a lantern festival called Loy Krathong Festival, which falls on the night of December 15th in the Thai calendar. It is said that Loy Krathong Festival began in the Sukhothai period, the first Thai Dynasty in the 13th century and then spread from the palace into the folk life. Floating the water lanterns, the main activity of the festival, originated as a memorial for the water god and gradually developed into a cheerful festival for celebrating the harvest, to thank the river god, to look for ideal life partners (for young people), and to pray for lovers to get married. Water lanterns, which are a feast for eyes, are in various shapes like those of the lotus, the phoenix and pagoda. People always make a beautiful wish before setting afloat the lanterns which will drift into the distance together holding the wish.

中秋节
The Mid-Autumn Festival

中国古代有许多关于月亮的神话传说，其中与中秋节有关的是"嫦娥奔月"。传说，嫦娥是射日英雄后羿的妻子，为了使人们免除灾难，她吞食了不死药，飞升入月，成为月神。为了纪念嫦娥，就有了中秋拜月的习俗。因为中秋节在农历八月十五，正好是秋季的中间，所以也是中国人庆祝丰收、盼望团圆的节日。

In ancient China, there were many myths and legends about the moon, among which "the Goddess Chang'e Flying to the Moon" is related to the Mid-Autumn Festival. It is said that Chang'e, wife of the hero Houyi who shoots the sun, eats the elixir of immortality and becomes the goddess of the moon after flying onto it. The custom of worshipping the moon during the Mid-Autumn Festival appears in memory of Chang'e. As the Mid-Autumn Festival is on August 15th (lunar calendar), the middle of autumn, it is also a day for Chinese people to celebrate the harvest and hope for family reunion.

嫦娥奔月
The Goddess Chang'e Flying to the Moon

中秋节起源于古人对月亮的崇拜。中国古代把月亮尊为月神。早在周代（前 11 世纪—前 256），天子每年都要在秋天举行祭月仪式。祭祀的传统是春分祭日，夏至祭地，秋分祭月，冬至祭天。祭祀的场所分别设立在国都的东、北、西、南四个方向。随着中秋节的演变发展，祭月与拜月

The Mid-Autumn Festival originated from the worship of the moon by ancient people who adored the moon as a god. Back to the Zhou Dynasty (11th century BC-256 BC), the emperor held the rite of offering sacrifices to the moon in autumn every year. The tradition is to offer sacrifice to the sun during the Spring Equinox, to the earth during the Summer Solstice, to the

风俗从宫廷流入民间，并逐渐发展为以娱乐为主的赏月活动。

月饼是中秋节不可缺少的食品和礼品，代表着圆圆的月亮，象征着家人的团聚。中国各地的月饼在用料、调味、形状和工艺等方面有不少差别，在月饼制作上形成了不同风格。传统中式月饼主要分为广式（广东）月饼、苏式（苏州）月饼、京式（北京）月饼三大类。20 世纪 90 年代以来，随着中国社会经济的发展，不少城市还出现了西式月饼，月饼的种类越来越丰富。

月饼
Mooncake

除月饼外，老北京的兔儿爷也很值得一提。兔儿爷是中秋应节应令的儿童玩具，初现于明代（1368—1644），盛行于清代（1616—1911）。人们按照月宫里有嫦娥、玉兔的说法，把玉兔进一步艺术化、人格化乃至神化，用泥巴制作出各种不同样式的塑像，大的可达 1 米，小的仅有 15 厘米。

moon during the Autumnal Equinox, and to the heaven during the Winter Solstice. The sacrifice takes place respectively in the east, north, west and south of the capital. With the development of the Mid-Autumn Festival, the custom of offering sacrifice and worshipping the moon spread from the palace into the folk culture and was gradually transformed into enjoying the moon mainly for entertainment reasons.

As an indispensible food and gift in the Mid-Autumn Festival, the mooncake represents the full moon and family reunion. Mooncakes in various areas of China differ from each other in terms of ingredients, condiments, shapes and production process, thus forming different styles of mooncake manufacturing. Traditional Chinese mooncakes mainly include Cantonese mooncakes, Suzhou mooncakes, and Beijing mooncakes. Since the 1990s, the social and economic development in China also contributed to the emergence of Western-style mooncakes and the great variety of mooncakes.

Besides the mooncakes, the clay rabbit of old Beijing is also worth mentioning. As a children's toy appropriate for the Mid-Autumn Festival, the clay rabbit appeared in the Ming Dynasty (1368-1644) and prevailed in the Qing Dynasty (1616-1911). Based on the story of Chang'e and the jade hare in the moon palace, people made the jade hare more artistic and even personalized and deified it. Various styles of statues made of mud can be as big as one meter or as small as 15 centimeters. The clay rabbit is rabbit-headed and human-bodied. Some sit up or stand solemnly wearing clothes and hats while some others wear helmets and

兔儿爷一般是兔首人身，有的穿衣戴帽，端坐或肃立；有的头戴金盔，身披战袍，背插旗帜，骑在虎、鹿、狮子、骆驼等动物上面。兔儿爷的形象极其憨厚可爱，使北京城的中秋节更加具有节日气氛。

北京兔儿爷，舒燕摄
Beijing clay rabbit, photographed by Shu Yan

在中国南方，如广西、四川等盛产柚子的地方，人们在过中秋节时常常制作柚子灯笼，即把柚子镂空，在里面点上蜡烛，作为孩子们的中秋玩具。在一些少数民族地区，人们在中秋节时还要以对唱情歌的浪漫方式寻觅佳偶。

此外，中秋节也是一个人们可以亲近自然、近距离感受大自然力量的节日。在浙江省钱塘地区，每年中秋节人们除了赏月外，还要去钱塘江边观看一年一度的钱塘江大潮。钱塘江大潮是由于月球和太阳引潮力的作用，在杭州湾喇叭口的特殊地形下形

coat armor with flags on their back, riding on tigers, deers, lions, camels and other animals. The clay rabbit looks quite simple, honest and cute, adding festive atmosphere to the Mid-Autumn Festival in Beijing.

In Guangxi Province, Sichuan Province and other places abounding in grapefruit in Southern China, people always make grapefruit lanterns as a children's toy during the Mid-Autumn Festival by hollowing out the grapefruit and lighting a candle in it. In some minority areas, people also look for good mates in a romantic way by singing love songs to one another during the festival.

Moreover, the Mid-Autumn Festival also offers an opportunity for people to get close to nature and experience the power of nature at short range. In the Qiantang area of Zhejiang Province, people will not only admire the moon but also watch the annual Qiantang River Tide by the Qiantang River during the festival. The Qiantang River Tide is an astronomical tide stemming from the special topography of

柚子灯
A grapefruit lantern

钱塘潮　　*Qiantang River Tide*

成的特大潮汐现象。每年农历八月十八涌潮最大，声如雷鸣，非常壮观。在钱塘江观潮的活动古已有之，后来成为当地特有的中秋习俗。

　　中秋节代表着中国人对月亮的独特情感，体现了中国家庭重视人伦、亲情与自然的文化传统。在中秋节的发展演变过程中，古老的神话传说与各地的中秋习俗结合在一起，为节日活动增添了诗意与浪漫色彩。

funnel-shaped Hangzhou Bay as a result of the tide generating force of the moon and the sun. The tide reaches its peak every lunar August 18th with thunderous sound and spectacular view. Watching the Qiantang River Tide can be traced back to ancient times and has become a Mid-Autumn Festival custom full of regional character.

The Mid-Autumn Festival represents Chinese people's special feelings for the moon and it reflects the Chinese cultural tradition of Chinese families valuing human relations, family affection and nature. In the evolution of the festival, ancient myths and legends, together with festival customs in various places, have made the festival activities more poetic and romantic.

中秋节时我们赏月、拜月、吃月饼，明月千里寄相思，这是中国人传统的表达感情与亲情的方式。现在有些礼数虽然淡化了，但秋高气爽之时尽享天伦之乐的习俗仍在。我觉得像中秋节这样的传统节日应该受到重视，因为它能让国人找到对自己民族文化的认同感。

[中国] 李惠芳，女，主持人

中秋节是一个团圆的节日，月圆、饼圆、桌圆、家圆，圆是中秋的主题。现在对于生活在城市的人来说，似乎已经鲜有机会像古人一样有全家逢中秋赏月看花的闲情雅致，甚至少有机会同家人坐在一起吃饭闲谈，但中秋节依然给我们团圆的机会，给我们家庭乃至民族凝聚的力量。

[中国] 于飞，男，研究生

During the Mid-Autumn Festival, we, believing that the bright moonlight is able to send love-sickness from a great distance, enjoy and worship the moon, and we eat mooncakes, which is a traditional way for Chinese people to express their emotions and family love. At present, despite the fading-out of some etiquette, the custom of enjoying family love during the crisp autumn weather remains. I think that traditional festivals like the Mid-Autumn Festival should be emphasized because they can help Chinese people gain more recognition of national cultural identity.

[China] Li Huifang, female, hostess

The Mid-Autumn Festival is a festival with the theme of reunion featuring full moon, mooncake, a round table and a family reunion. Now for people living in urban areas, there are few opportunities to have the leisure and interest to admire the moon and flowers with the whole family during the Mid-Autumn Festival. They even do not have much time to eat and chat with their family members. However, the Mid-Autumn Festival still provides us with the opportunity for families to get together as well as the power to unify the family and even the nation.

[China] Yu Fei, male, graduate student

古希腊神话中的月亮女神阿蒂米斯（Artemis），是太阳神阿波罗的妹妹。她不仅非常漂亮，而且是个很出色的弓箭手。每天她驾着银色的马车在夜空中奔驰，身边伴随着心爱的弓箭和猎犬。她掌管着狩猎，同时，她也是未婚少女的守护神。

The moon goddess Artemis in ancient Greek my-thology is the sister of Apollo, the sun god. As an excellent archer with beautiful appearance, she gallops in the night sky on her silver carriage, accompanied by her beloved bows, arrows and hound. She is in charge of hunting. She is also the patroness of unmarried girls.

古希腊月亮女神
The moon goddess in ancient Greek

Traditional Customs

传统习俗

生日习俗
Birthday Conventions

导入 INTRODUCTION

中国人一向重视传宗接代，因此都喜欢《百子图》。"百"含有大或者无穷的意思，《百子图》把祝福、恭贺的良好愿望发挥到了极致。"子孙满堂"被认为是家族兴旺的最主要的表现，《百子图》寓意多福多寿，多子多孙，子孙昌盛，万代延续。由于传统上对出生的重视，中国人特别重视生日。

Chinese people always attach importance to the continuation of the family line and therefore love *The Picture of A Hundred Children* very much. As "one hundred" can imply largeness and infiniteness, *The Picture of A Hundred Children* fully embodies good wishes, blessings and congratulations. "Sons and grandsons pervading the hall" is regarded as the main reflection of a prosperous family. *The Picture of a Hundred Children* implies good fortune, longevity, fertility, prosperity of descendants, and continuation of the family line. As a result of the traditional emphasis on birth, Chinese people value birthdays very much.

用《百子图》局部画面装饰的笔筒，田琨摄

Pen holder decorated with a part of The Picture of A Hundred Children, photographed by Tian Kun

中国人过生日的习俗兴起于魏晋（220—420），唐宋（618—1279）以后大盛。在一个家庭中，孩子和老人的生日最为重要。

婴儿出生满一个月称为"满月"，这一天有一项重要的仪俗活动——剃胎发，这是新生儿出生后第一次理发。

The convention of Chinese people to celebrate birthdays began in the Wei and Jin dynasties (220-420) and prevailed until after the Tang and Song dynasties (618-1279). In a family, the birthdays of children and the aged are of the greatest importance.

A baby's completion of the first month of life is called *man yue* when the newborn gets his

新生儿的胎发受之于父母，因此剃胎发在中国各地都格外受重视。剃下来的胎发不能随便扔掉，而是要放在一起，用丝线缠好，由母亲挂在孩子床头，据说可以保佑孩子平安成长。

"过百岁"是婴儿出生一百天的庆贺仪式，希望孩子能长命百岁。人们可以送婴儿长命锁作为礼物。长命锁一般是用金银打造的，上有"长命百岁"、"长命富贵"等字样，用链子挂在孩子脖子上，垂在胸前。

婴儿出生满一年称为"周岁"。按照传统习俗，这一天要举行"抓周"仪式。父母把弓箭、珍宝、玩器、针线、文房书籍等东西摆在婴儿前面，让婴儿自由抓取，以最先抓取的为有效，人们通过这种方法来预测孩子的性情、志趣和前途。比如孩子先抓起来的是书，就认为孩子将来能专心做学问。"抓周"最早见于南北朝时期，

抓周，郑炜摄
Choosing one object among many others, photographed by Zheng Wei

or her fetal hair cut for the first time after birth, which is an important convention. Since the fetal hair is received from the parents, cutting the fetal hair is particularly emphasized all around China. The shaved fetal hair cannot be randomly thrown away but should be put together and bound by silk threads. Then the mother should hang it above the baby's bed, which is allegedly able to bless the baby to grow up safely.

People also celebrate the one hundredth day after the birth of the baby, hoping that the baby lives to a ripe old age. The longevity lock, a gift made of gold and silver with "长命百岁" (life of a hundred years) and "长命富贵" (longevity with wealth and honor) on it, is hung on the baby's neck with a chain and falls onto the chest.

One full year of life of the baby is called *zhousui* on which day, according to traditional customs, the baby has to choose one object among many others that will symbolize his or her future. Parents will put bows, arrows, treasures, toys, needleworks, and books before the baby so that he or she can grab anything freely. Then the parents will make their judgments according to the first object grabbed by the baby. In this way, people can predict the baby's temperament, interest and future. The convention of choosing one object among many others originated from the Southern and Northern dynasties. Nowadays, the custom is still seen in many places, but most people only regard it as entertaining.

现在尽管很多地方仍存在"抓周"的习俗，但人们一般仅仅把"抓周"看作是一项娱乐活动。

年轻人过生日比较随意。随着生活节奏的加快，人们也越来越喜欢找些理由给自己放假，其中过生日就是最好的借口之一。生日那天，不仅能收到生日礼物与祝福，还能与亲朋好友聚在一起，点生日蜡烛，吃生日蛋糕，唱《生日快乐》歌，心里甭提多高兴了。此外，在信息时代的今天，给亲朋好友发送一张电子贺卡庆祝生日也成了一种时髦的方式。

生日蛋糕，田琨摄
Birthday cake, photographed by Tian Kun

祝寿是中国各民族普遍的习俗。民间以 60 岁为寿年，60 岁以下或父母健在的人一般不能称寿，只能叫生日。老人一入寿年，子女、亲朋便要进行生日的庆祝活动，俗称"祝寿"。

Young people celebrate birthdays at their will. As the pace of life quickens, people increasingly tend to find excuses for a holiday and to celebrate the birthday is one of the best excuses. On the birthday, one will not only receive birthday gifts and blessings but also get together with relatives and friends, lighting the birthday candles, eating birthday cakes and singing the "Happy Birthday Song" in great delight. In addition, in the information age, it is also fashionable to celebrate the birthday of relatives and friends by sending an electronic greeting card to them.

Offering birthday congratulations to elderly people is a common convention among different ethnic groups in China. The age of 60 is regarded as the age of longevity and those under 60 or those whose parents are in good health can only celebrate their birthday, but not longevity. After one becomes more than 60 years old, his or her children, relatives and friends will offer birthday congratulations, known as *zhushou*. Birthday noodles and peach-shaped cakes are traditional objects representing good luck. The eating of birthday noodles is referred to as *tiao shou*, meaning happiness and longevity. Peach-shaped cakes are not real peaches but peach-shaped steam buns made of leavened dough with the character " 寿 " (longevity) in red written on it. The most commonly used words to offer birthday congratulations are " 福如东海寿比南山 " (may your happiness be as boundless as the eastern seas and your life as

寿面、寿桃是传统习俗中用于祝寿的吉祥物品，吃寿面叫"挑寿"，喻意福寿延绵。寿桃其实不是真正的桃子，而是一种用发面蒸的桃形馒头，"桃"身写有红色的"寿"字。祝寿时最常说的祝寿语是"福如东海，寿比南山"，希望老人长命百岁。

long as the long lasting southern mountains), expressing the wish that elderly people can live a hundred years.

福禄寿三星祝寿图
The Picture of Luck, Prosperity and Longevity Offering Birthday Congratulations

三言两语 A FEW REMARKS

11月28日是我儿子的生日。他和我们一起在丹麦生活，已经在丹麦过了两个生日了。每年他都热切地盼望着生日这天早日到来，因为这一天，他在幼儿园是最受重视和瞩目的孩子。生日当天，一到幼儿园，老师就会为他升起一面丹麦国旗。这样，所有小朋友和家长就知道了，今天有个小朋友过生日。大家也会向他表示祝贺，那天的活

November 28th is my son's birthday. He lives with us in Denmark and has had two birthdays there. Every year he keenly looks forward to the coming of that day when he gets the most attention in the school. On his birthday, as soon as he arrives at school, his teacher will raise the Denmark flag for him so that his schoolmates and their parents will know that this day is somebody's birthday and to congratulate him on his birthday. He will also become the focus of all activities on that day.

动也会围绕他进行。

[中国] 顾文娟，女，公司职员

我儿子过周岁生日的时候，我和他爸爸在他周围放了好多东西，硬币啊、书啊、笔啊什么的，最后他抓了一个计算器。我和他爸爸一看，这以后是要当会计啊，和数字打交道。你别说，这抓周还挺准的。他现在非常喜欢数字，楼号、车牌号，只要看到都会读出来。其实孩子以后干什么都不重要，只要他能平平安安、快快乐乐地生活我就满足了。

[中国] 陈梦，女，家庭主妇

[China] Gu Wenjuan, female, company employee

When my son had his first birthday, his father and I put many things before him such as coins, books and pens. At last, he picked up a calculator. His father and I saw that and thought he would become an accountant dealing with numbers in the future. Believe it or not, our guess is right. Now he loves numbers so much that he will read out building numbers and license plate numbers as soon as he sees them. In fact, his job in the future is not quite important for me because I will be satisfied as long as he lives safely and happily.

[China] Chen Meng, female, housewife

小链接 ADDITIONAL INFORMATION

生日人人都有，但由于各国历史和文化不同，对待生日礼物中西方国家的处理方式大相径庭。如果是中国人，主人一般不会当着客人的面打开礼物，否则会让大家觉得主人是个好计较、气量小的人，还可能因礼物分量大小而使客人难堪，所以当着客人的面打开礼物是失礼的行为。而西方人则不同，总是当着客人的面打开礼物欣赏。他们认为这样做是表示礼貌，说明主人很喜欢客人送的礼物，而客人也会感到欣慰，认为自己受到了尊重。

Although everybody has his or her birthday, the convention of handling birthday gifts is quite different in China from that in Western countries due to their different history and culture. Chinese people do not open the gift before the giver for they do not want to appear to be calculating and narrow-minded or embarrass the giver because of the value of the gift. For Chinese people, unwrapping the gift in the presence of the giver is quite impolite. Western people, however, do not think so. They usually open the gift for admiration in front of the giver, which, in their mind, is a polite way to show their love for the gift and will make the giver feel delighted and respected.

生肖动物
Zodiac Animals

这是十二生肖中的马，那么猜一猜下面这些谜语的谜底是十二生肖中的什么动物？1、走起路来落梅花，从早到晚守着家，看见生人就想咬，看见主人摇尾巴。2、年纪并不大，胡子一大把，最爱吃青草，喜欢叫妈妈。3、红红眼睛白白毛，长长耳朵短尾翘，身披一件白皮袄，走起路来轻轻跳。

This is the horse of the twelve zodiac animals. Let us guess which animals among the twelve zodiac animals are the answers to the following riddles: 1.Walks with plum blossom-shaped footprints, keeps guard of the house from day to night, bites at sight of any strangers, and wags the tail at sight of the master. 2. Although at an early age, it has a long beard, loves to eat green grass most, and always likes to call for "mama". 3. It has red eyes and white hair, as well as long ears and a short tail; it has a white fur-lined coat, and it bounces around vivaciously.

十二生肖中的马，刘谦功摄
Horse of the twelve zodiac animals, photographed by Liu Qiangong

十二生肖是中国传统文化的重要组成部分，用于纪年，由鼠、牛、虎、兔、龙、蛇、马、羊、猴、鸡、狗、猪十二种动物组成，其中龙是人们想象中的动物。十二生肖与中国传统的十二地支①相配合，形成子鼠、丑牛、寅虎、卯兔、辰龙、巳蛇、午马、未羊、

As an important part of Chinese traditional culture, the twelve zodiac signs are made up of the mouse, the ox, the tiger, the rabbit, the dragon, the snake, the horse, the sheep, the monkey, the rooster, the dog and the pig, among which the dragon is an imaginary one. The twelve zodiac signs correspond to the Chinese traditional Twelve Earthly Branches [1],

---

① 地支：天干地支简称"干支"。在中国古代历法中，甲、乙、丙、丁、戊、己、庚、辛、壬、癸被称为"十天干"，子、丑、寅、卯、辰、巳、午、未、申、酉、戌、亥被称为"十二地支"。十干和十二支依次相配，组成六十个基本单位，两者按固定的顺序互相配合，组成了干支纪法，用于纪年、纪月、纪日、纪时等。

① The Twelve Earthly Branches: the Heavenly Stems and the Earthly Branches are called Stems-and-Branches in short. In Chinese traditional calendar, *jia, yi, bing, ding, wu, ji, geng, xin, ren, gui* are called the Ten Heavenly Stems and *zi, chou, yin, mao, chen, si, wu, wei, shen, you, xu, hai* are called the Twelve Earthly Branches. The Ten Heavenly Stems and the Twelve Earthly Branches match up with each other in fixed order and form sixty basic units, thus producing the Chinese sexagenarian cycle used to name the year, month, day, and hour.

申猴、酉鸡、戌狗、亥猪的排列顺序。

十二生肖罗盘
The compass of the twelve zodiac signs

据说，十二生肖的选用与排列是根据动物每天的活动时间确定的，所以生肖之间不能随便变换顺序。中国至迟从汉代开始用十二地支记录一天的十二个时辰，每个时辰相当于两个小时。夜晚十一时到凌晨一时是子时，老鼠最为活跃；一时到三时是丑时，牛正在反刍；三时到五时是寅时，老虎正在到处觅食，最为凶猛；五时到七时是卯时，月亮还挂在天上，玉兔正忙着捣药①；上午七时到九时是辰时，是神龙行雨②的好时光；九时到十一时是巳时，蛇开始活跃起来；上午十一时到下午一时是午时，阳气正盛，是天马行空的时候；一时到三时是未时，羊在这时吃草会长得更壮；三时到五时是申时，猴子最为活跃；

forming the order of *zishu* (mouse), *chouniu* (ox), *yinhu* (tiger), *maotu* (rabbit), *chenlong* (dragon), *sishe* (snake), *wuma* (horse), *weiyang* (sheep), *shenhou* (monkey), *youji* (rooster), *xugou* (dog) and *haizhu* (pig).

It is said that the selection and the order of the twelve zodiac signs are based on the time table of the animals and the order cannot be changed randomly. Chinese people used the Twelve Earthly Branches no later than the Han Dynasty to record the 12 *shichen* every day (each *shichen* equals to two hours). The period of the day from 11 pm to 1 am is *zishi* when the mouse is the most active. One to three in the morning is *choushi* when the ox is ruminating. Three to five in the morning is *yinshi* when the fiercest tiger is looking around for food. Five to seven in the morning is *maoshi* when the jade hare is busy with making medicine with the moon still in the sky[1]. Seven to nine in the morning is *chenshi*, good time for the dragon king to bring rain to the world[2]. Nine to eleven in the morning is *sishi* when the snake becomes active. 11 am to 1 pm is *wushi* when Yang is at its highest and the heavenly steed soars across the skies. One to three in the afternoon is *weishi* when the sheep eats grass to grow stronger. Three to five in the afternoon is *shenshi* when the monkey is the most active. Five to seven in the afternoon is *youshi* when the night falls and the rooster returns to its shelter. Seven to nine in the evening is *xushi* when the dog keeps watch at night. Nine to eleven in

---

① 玉兔捣药：相传月亮之中有一只兔子，浑身洁白如玉，所以被称作"玉兔"。玉兔拿着玉杵跪地捣药，制成蛤蟆丸，服后可以长生成仙。

② 神龙行雨：民间认为龙王掌管着雨水，一旦久旱不雨，人们便请出龙王，祭祀求雨。现在许多地方仍保留着祭龙祈雨这一习俗。

① The jade hare makes medicine: it is said that on the moon lives a hare called the Jade Hare which is as white as polished jade. Falling on its knees with a jade pestle, it makes the medicine of toad pill which enables one to become immortal.

② The dragon king brings rain to the world: ordinary people think that the dragon king is in charge of rain. When suffering from longtime drought, people will offer sacrifices to the dragon king for rain. This custom remains in many places nowadays.

五时到七时是酉时，夜幕降临，鸡开始归窝；晚上七时到九时是戌时，狗开始守夜；九时到十一时是亥时，万籁俱寂，猪正在鼾睡。

知道了十二生肖的排列顺序以后，你就能判断哪一年是什么年了。比如 2005 年是鸡年，那么你就能知道 2004 年是猴年，2006 年是狗年。而且只要知道了一个年份的生肖，你也可以通过加减 12 的办法，算出过去和未来属相相同的年是哪些年了。比如 2005 年是鸡年，那么 2005 加或减 12 的倍数的年，如 2017 年、1993 年也都是鸡年。

唐代辰蛇生肖石刻
The stone sculpture of the zodiac animal snake in the Tang Dynasty

在十二生肖中，龙是唯一一种想象中的动物。它在中国文化中是幸运、吉祥的化身，也正因如此，现在许多年轻人都喜欢扎堆在龙年生孩子，因为龙年出生的孩子是"龙子"。

十二生肖剪纸
Papercuts of the twelve zodiac signs

the evening is *haishi* when the pig is sleeping soundly in prevailing silence.

If you grasp the order of those twelve animals, you can know the zodiac animal of a certain year. For instance, 2005 is the year of the rooster, and then you can figure out that 2004 is the year of the monkey and 2006 is the year of the dog. If you know the zodiac sign of the year, you can add or subtract twelve to find the years of the same zodiac sign in the future and in the past. For example, 2005 is the year of the rooster, and years of 2005 plus or minus 12 as well as multiples of 12 such as 2017 and 1993 are also years of the rooster.

Among the twelve zodiac signs, the dragon is the only imaginary animal. Due to its representation of good luck in Chinese culture, many young people at present prefer to give birth to their babies in the year of the dragon because those born at that time are "the sons of the dragon".

There are a variety of good-looking cultural

现在以十二生肖为主要内容的文化产品十分丰富，比如剪纸、年画、邮票等等，设计精美，色彩鲜艳，看着特别养眼。

products concerning the twelve zodiac signs such as paper-cuts, New Year pictures and stamps with delicate design and bright color.

三言两语 A FEW REMARKS

你要问我十二生肖里最喜欢什么动物，我最喜欢狗，因为我属狗。属狗的人直率、诚实，为人仗义，好打抱不平，朋友们都是这么评价我的。我觉得从属相看性格还挺准的：我爸属马，性格开朗，但有时候有点儿暴躁；我妈属猪，非常勤劳，心地善良。外国有星座，中国有属相，挺有意思的。

[中国] 陈婷，女，公司职员

按照中国的属相我属兔。几年前，我的一个中国朋友送给我一张兔年的生肖邮票，我特别喜欢。从那以后，每年我都会在中国人过春节的时候到邮局买新的生肖邮票来收藏。我班里的学生们对十二生肖也很感兴趣，他们都知道自己的属相。

[美国] 温妮，女，小学教师

When asked about my favorite animal among the twelve zodiac signs, I would answer that I love the dog most because I was born in the year of the dog. Those born in years of the dog are straightforward and honest and love to uphold justice. My friends all comment on me in this way. In my opinion, the zodiac sign indicates one's character. My father, born in the year of the horse, is cheerful but irritable sometimes while my mother, born in the year of the pig, is quite diligent and kind. It is quite interesting that China uses zodiac signs and Western countries use horoscopes.
[China] Chen Ting, female, company employee

I was born in the year of the rabbit according to Chinese zodiac signs. A few years ago, one of my Chinese friends gave me a stamp for the year of the rabbit which delighted me a lot. From then on, I would buy zodiac-themed stamps in the post office every Chinese Spring Festival. The students in my class are also interested in the twelve zodiac signs and all know their own zodiac signs.
[US] Winnie, female, primary school teacher

小链接
ADDITIONAL INFORMATION

越南也有十二生肖，它们是鼠、牛、虎、猫、龙、蛇、马、羊、猴、鸡、狗和猪。其中十一个与中国生肖一样，只是越南有"猫"而无"兔"，此外排列顺序也与中国生肖相同。越南的十二生肖最早是从中国传入的，那为什么中国的"兔"到了越南变成"猫"了呢？一种说法是，当时中国的生肖纪年法传入越南时，"卯兔"的"卯"与"猫"的读音相似，结果"卯年"误读成"猫年"；另一种说法是，当时越南尚无"兔"这种动物，因此就用"猫"来代替"兔"了。

Vietnam also has twelve zodiac signs—the mouse, the ox, the tiger, the cat, the dragon, the snake, the horse, the sheep, the monkey, the rooster, the dog and the pig. Eleven of them are the same with Chinese zodiac signs and Vietnam has the sign of the "cat" but not the "rabbit". The order of the zodiac signs is also the same with China. The twelve zodiac signs in Vietnam were originally introduced from China. Yet why the "rabbit" in China become the "cat" in Vietnam? Some people say that when the zodiac signs used to record the year were introduced to Vietnam the pronunciation of *maotu* (rabbit) in Chinese is similar to that of *mao* (cat) in Vietnamese. As a result, *maonian* (the year of the rabbit) was read as *maonian* (the year of the cat). Some others say that "cat" was used to replace "rabbit" because at that time Vietnam had no rabbits.

中国龙
Chinese Dragon

导入 INTRODUCTION

"……古老的东方有一条龙，它的名字就叫中国。古老的东方有一群人，他们全都是龙的传人。巨龙脚底下我成长，长成以后是龙的传人，黑眼睛、黑头发、黄皮肤，永永远远是龙的传人……"这首歌的名字叫《龙的传人》。为什么有"中国龙"的说法，中国人又为什么被称为"龙的传人"？

"...In the ancient East there is a dragon called by the name of China. In the ancient East there are a group of people who are the descendants of the dragon. Growing up under the foot of the huge dragon, they, with black eyes, black hair and yellow skin, are forever the descendants of the dragon..." The name of this song is "Descendants of the Dragon". Why China is called a dragon and Chinese people are called "descendants of the dragon"?

上海豫园的龙头墙，田琨摄
The dragon head wall in Yu Garden in Shanghai, photographed by Tian Kun

在中国神话里，始祖神女娲与伏羲均为人首蛇身的形象。在华夏民族的祖先统一了中原各部落以后，糅合了各氏族的图腾，形成了龙的形象。现在人们看到的龙的形象主要是——鹿角、牛耳、驼头、兔眼、蛇颈、蜃腹、鱼鳞、虎掌、鹰爪，完全是人们想象的，并非自然界真实存在的动物。

In Chinese mythology, the ancestor goddess Nuwa and god Fuxi are human-headed and snake-bodied. After the ancestors of the Chinese nation unified the tribes along the Yellow River, the image of the dragon was formed based on the combination of the totem images of all the clans. At present, people think that the dragon is made up of deer horns, ox ears, a camel head, rabbit eyes, a

龙作为一种神物具有掌管雨水的神性，因而人们很早就把龙当作水神进行崇拜，建了很多龙神庙或龙王庙，都是用来祈雨的。

龙形图案
Dragon-shaped image

在中国封建社会，龙一直是皇帝和皇权的象征。早在春秋战国时期（前770—前221），人们就开始把有本领、有作为的人比作龙。秦朝末年，人们也曾把秦始皇称为"祖龙"。西汉初年，社会上流行刘媪因蛟龙附体而孕生刘邦的说法。因此历代皇帝都自称"真龙天子"，其长相称"龙颜"，身体是"龙体"，衣服叫"龙袍"……凡皇帝用的东西都冠上一个"龙"字。他们甚至垄断龙纹，只许自己使用，据说在清代皇宫的主殿太和殿里就装饰有大大小小的12654条龙。

snake neck, a clam abdomen, with fish scales and tiger paws and eagle claws. The dragon is completely imagined by people and does not exist in nature.

As a mythic creature in charge of the rain, dragons are adored as the rain god by people who build many temples of the dragon god and the dragon king to pray for rain.

In feudal society in China, dragons always symbolize the emperor and his power. Back during the Spring and Autumn Period and Warring States Period (770 BC-221 BC), people began to compare competent and accomplished people to dragons. At the end of the Qin Dynasty, the first emperor of Qin was called "the first dragon". During the early Western Han Dynasty, there was a widespread belief that Liu Ao gave birth to Liu Bang after being possessed by the dragon. Therefore, all emperors call themselves sons of heaven with "dragon-like appearances" and "dragon-like bodies" wearing "dragon robes". Everything used by the emperors would be called the thing of the dragon. They allowed nobody but themselves to use the dragon design. It is said that the Hall of Supreme Harmony, the main hall in the imperial palace of the Qing Dynasty, was decorated with 12,654 dragons in various sizes.

龙袍（中华民族艺术珍品博物馆馆藏）
The dragon robe (reserved in Chinese National Art Treasure Museum)

　　在中国的传统节日中，有不少与龙有关，比如农历二月二是"龙抬头"的节日。此时正值惊蛰、春分时节，民俗认为蛰伏一冬的龙要在这一天抬头活动，即意味着以后的雨水要逐渐多起来了。此外，农历五月初五为"端午节"，赛龙舟是其中一项重要的民俗活动。

Many Chinese traditional festivals are related to the dragon. For instance, February 2nd of the lunar calendar, the day when the dragon raises its head, is during the time of the Waking of Insects and the Spring Equinox. People believe that this is when the dragon raises its head after the winter hibernation, meaning that there will be more rain following. In addition, May 5th of the lunar calendar is the Dragon Boat Festival when dragon-boat racing is amongst the most important of folk activities.

In modern society, the dragon worshipped as something sacred in the past has become a mascot or a sign of good luck. The dragon, containing the meanings of rising rapidly with spirit and force, pioneering spirit and changes, embodies the spirit of being energetic and making progress. During festivals, we can always see the teams of dragon dance and

舞龙　　*The dragon dance*

进入现代社会以后，过去一直被当作神物崇拜的龙，更多地变为一种吉祥物或吉祥符号。龙有腾飞、振奋、开拓、变化等寓意，因此龙的精神也就是昂扬向上的精神。逢年过节我们经常能看到舞龙的队伍，实实在在地让人们感到龙腾虎跃的气派。

在中华大地上，我们到处可以看到龙。从划龙舟、舞龙灯，到龙的绘画、龙的雕刻、龙的旗帜，龙已经深深扎根于中国人的心中，成为中华民族的象征。20世纪80年代以来，《龙的传人》、《中国龙》等歌曲广为流传，中国人是"龙的传人"的说法深入人心。

truly feel the air of dragons rising and tigers leaping.

Across China's landscape, dragons can be witnessed everywhere. Deeply rooted in Chinese people's heart, they have become the symbol of the Chinese nation, as is reflected in dragon-boat racing, dragon lantern dance as well as paintings, sculptures, and flags of dragons. Since the 1980s, songs such as "Descendants of the Dragon" and "Chinese Dragon" have been widely circulated and it is deeply rooted in people's mind that Chinese people are the descendants of the dragon.

三言两语 A FEW REMARKS

中国的龙与西方的龙不管是从形象还是象征意义上来说都是不一样的。中国人认为龙是一种能兴云雨利万物的神异动物，在中国传统的十二生肖中排第五，并且与白虎、朱雀、玄武一起并称"四神兽"。佛家、道家均与龙有些渊源。在中国人心目中，龙始终有着特殊的地位。现在龙是吉祥的象征、力量的象征、朝气的象征，更是中华民族的象征。

[中国] 邹琳，女，研究生

提起龙，首先我联想到的就是中国。如果非要刨根问底它还会让我想起什么，我才会想到神话故事里的怪兽。有些中国人担心龙会让我们有不好的联想，其实没有必要。在我眼里它就是一个符号，不会有

Chinese dragons differ from Western dragons both in images and in symbolic meaning. In Chinese people's minds, the dragon is an extraordinary animal capable of bringing clouds and rain to benefit all creatures. As the fifth animal in the Chinese traditional zodiac animals, it is among the "four mythical creatures" together with the white tiger, the phoenix and the black tortoise. Buddhism and Taoism are both historically associated with the dragon. The dragon always has a special position in Chinese people's mind. Nowadays, the dragon represents good luck, power, vitality, as well as the Chinese nation.

[China] Zou Lin, female, graduate student

At the mentioning of a dragon, I would think about China first. If asked more about what I would think of, I would then say the monster in mythology. Some Chinese people are worried that dragons will be associated with

不好的感觉。我很喜欢舞龙的表演，我的朋友有的还在身上刺有龙的图案。

　　[法国] 让·菲利普，男，金融机构职员

something bad in our minds, but it is quite unnecessary. In my eyes, it is only a sign bringing no bad feelings. I love the dragon dance very much and one of my friends even has a dragon tattoo on his body.

　　[France] Jean Philippe, male, financial institution employee

小链接 ADDITIONAL INFORMATION

西方龙的形象
The image of a Western dragon

　　在中国人的印象中，龙具有神性，是祥瑞和中华民族文化的象征。但龙在世界各国所受欢迎的程度以及大家对它的印象可不完全相同。西方的龙被认为是邪恶的魔兽，是撒旦的使者。它身形巨大，口吐烈火，背上有两片大翅膀，人们常常被它吃掉。日本人的龙的造型跟中国几乎一样，只是它是忍术的象征，他们的忍者常在身上刺龙的图案，从一部卡通《双截龙》就可以明显看出龙在日本人心目中的样子了。

In Chinese people's minds, the dragon is divine and symbolic of Chinese culture as an auspicious sign. However, the dragon varies considerably in terms of popularity and people's impressions of it all over the world. With a huge body and two large wings on its back, the Western dragon, able to spit raging fire, is regarded as an evil monster and the messenger of Satan. In Japan, the dragon has a similar image with that in China but represents Ninjutsu. The ninja in Japan often have dragon tattoos. The image of the dragon in Japanese people's minds can be seen clearly in the cartoon "Double Dragon".

Chinese Arts

中国艺术

京 剧
Beijing Opera

　　梅兰芳是中国杰出的京剧表演艺术家，1930 年曾率团访问美国，第一次将神奇的东方戏剧展现在西方人面前。梅剧团先后在华盛顿、芝加哥、洛杉矶等地演出了 72 天，大受欢迎。由于人们特别推崇梅兰芳，美国波摩拿学院、南加利福尼亚大学分别授予其文学荣誉博士学位。

Mei Lanfang, an excellent performing artist of Beijing Opera in China, headed an opera troupe to America in 1930 and presented a magical Eastern opera performance before Western people. The opera troupe won great popularity through its 72-day performance in

梅兰芳 1930 年赴美演出剧照
Stage photo of Mei Lanfang in America in 1930

places such as Washington, Chicago and Los Angeles. Out of the admiration of Mei Lanfang, Pomona College and the University of Southern California granted him the honorary Doctor of Literature Degree.

　　京剧诞生于中国历史上最后一个封建王朝——清朝，乾隆五十五年（1790），为庆祝乾隆皇帝寿辰，许多地方戏班进京演出，最受欢迎的是来自安徽的四大戏班——三庆班、四喜班、和春班、春台班，他们以独特的艺术风格和精湛的表演技艺打动了朝野上下各阶层观众的

Beijing Opera appeared in the Qing Dynasty, the last feudal dynasty in Chinese history. In the 55th year of the Emperor Qianlong (1790), many opera troupes went to Beijing for performances to celebrate the birthday of the emperor. The most popular ones were the four opera troupes from Anhui—Sanqing Troupe, Sixi Troupe, Hechun Troupe and Chuntai Troupe. With unique artistic style and exquisite

心。在北京期间，四大徽班在徽剧
的基础上吸收了其他剧种如秦腔、
昆曲、汉剧等的长处创立了一个新
剧种——京剧。在没有电影与电视
的时代，听戏成为人们生活中不可
或缺的一项内容，更有划时代意义
的是，中国电影即诞生于 1905 年拍
摄京剧《定军山》①。

京剧《定军山》拍摄地——前门大观楼，田琨摄
Daguanlou Cinema in Qianming—the filming location of the Beijing Opera Dingjun Mountain, photographed by Tian Kun

在京剧成形与发展的过程中，清
朝同治与光绪年间十三位著名演员发
挥了很大的作用，被称为"同光十三
绝"，他们演出的剧目与饰演的角色
至今仍是中国京剧的经典。当时的画
师沈容圃描绘了他们的戏装像，其中
饰演《雁门关》中萧太后的梅巧玲就

performance, they touched the hearts of the audience from all walks of life, government officials and ordinary people alike. While in Beijing, the four Anhui troupes created a new type of opera—Beijing Opera on the basis of Anhui Opera and by absorbing the advantages of other operas such as Shaanxi Opera, Kunqu Opera and Hanchu Opera. During the time without movie and TV, going to the opera was an essential part of people's life. A more epoch-making event is that Chinese films came into being when people shot Beijing Opera *Dingjun Mountain* in 1905.①

During the formation and development of Beijing Opera, thirteen famous actors, known as *Tongguang Shisan Jue* during the reign of Emperor Tongzhi and Emperor Guangxu in the Qing Dynasty made a lot of contributions. Their plays and roles are still classic even at present. Shen Rongpu, a painter during that time, drew their portraits in costumes. Among them, Mei Qiaoling, who played the part of Xiao Queen Mother in *Yanmen Pass*, is the grandfather of Mei Lanfang.

Beijing Opera is quite unique in role shaping because it divides the roles into different categories according to their gender, age, identity and character in order to represent

[清]沈容圃《同光十三绝》（北京湖广会馆戏剧博物馆藏）

[Qing Dynasty] Shen Rongpu, Togguang Shisan Jue (reserved in Beijing Huguang Guild Hall, an opera museum)

① 中国电影的诞生：1905 年，中国人尝试拍摄电影，主持人是北京丰泰照相馆的创办人任景丰，摄影师是照相技师刘仲伦，拍摄了由著名京剧演员谭鑫培主演的《定军山》片段，这是中国人自己摄制的第一部电影。

① The birth of Chinese films: in 1905, Chinese people tried to shoot a film hosted by Ren Jingfeng, founder of Beijing Fengtai Photo Studio, and it was shot by Liu Zhonglun, a photographer. They shot a part of *Dingjun Mountain* starring Tan Xinpei, a famous Beijing Opera actor at the time. This was indeed the first film shot by Chinese people.

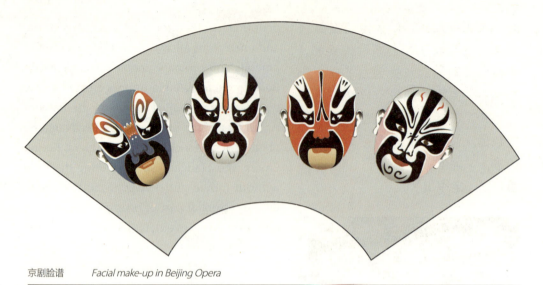

京剧脸谱　　*Facial make-up in Beijing Opera*

是梅兰芳的祖父。京剧在塑造人物方面有其独特之处，即按照不同性别、年龄、身份、性格将人物划分为不同行当，代表形形色色的人物。京剧行当分为生、旦、净、丑四大类，每个行当都有自己的造型特征和表演体系。"生"是男性角色，主要有老生、小生、武生等；"旦"是女性角色，主要有老旦、青衣、花旦、武旦等；"净"是个性鲜明、体态壮硕的男性角色，主要是英雄、将军、天神等；"丑"是喜剧角色，主要是滑稽或反面人物。在这些角色中，"净"的面部化妆最为著名，俗称"脸谱"。

　　有一首流行歌曲唱道："外国人把那京戏叫作 Beijing Opera。"① 其实京剧不是歌剧，歌剧只唱不说，事

various people. Beijing Opera has four types of roles—*sheng*, *dan*, *jing*, and *chou*, each of which has its own modeling feature and acting system. *Sheng* means male characters, mainly including *laosheng*, *xiaosheng* and *wusheng*. *Dan* represents female characters, mainly including *laodan*, *qingyi*, *huadan* and *wudan*. *Jing* means male characters with distinct personality and tough bodies such as hero, general and god. *Chou* is a comical role which is the mostly funny or negative character. Among these roles, the *Jing*s facial make-up is the most well-known and called *lianpu*.

A popular song goes like this, "Foreigners call *Jingxi* Beijing Opera."① In fact, Beijing Opera is different from opera, the latter telling the story and expressing the thoughts by singing instead of speaking while the former stresses

---

① 流行歌曲《唱脸谱》歌词，该歌曲由阎肃作词，姚明作曲，是一首京剧曲调跟流行音乐巧妙融合的歌曲。

① lyrics of the popular song "Song of *Lianpu*" composed by Yao Ming with the lyrics written by Yan Su. It ingeniously combines the tune of Beijing Opera and popular music.

件的叙述与思想的表达都是由歌唱形式完成的，而京剧则讲究"唱、念、做、打"。"唱"指歌唱，"念"指音乐性念白，"做"指舞蹈化动作，"打"指武打技艺。由此可见，京剧是一种综合性很强的戏剧艺术。

在京剧表演中，演员与观众的互动也是京剧艺术的魅力之一，过去京剧舞台多置于观众之中，台上唱戏，台下喝彩，台上台下一出戏，热闹非凡。现在京剧已成为中国的国粹与文化符号，直观地从一个侧面诠释了中国文化的博大精深。

chang, nian, zuo, da. Chang refers to singing, nian refers to musical spoken parts, zuo refers to dance movements and da refers to martial skills. Therefore, Beijing Opera is a comprehensive art.

In Beijing Opera performance, the interaction between the performers and the audience is also one of the charms of this art. In the past, the stage is often set within the audience. The performers act on stage and the audience cheer off stage, forming a scene of bustle and excitement. Today, Beijing Opera has become the quintessence and the sign of Chinese culture, directly reflecting the rich and profound Chinese culture from one perspective.

《霸王别姬》剧照　　Stage photo of Farewell My Concubine

三言两语 A FEW REMARKS

我小时候爱看武戏，热闹，后来才看文戏。看戏长知识，历史上好多事这里头都有，而且角色形象上就是非分明，是忠是奸一眼就能看出来。现在我上了年岁，更爱听文戏了，不光是这唱腔、这韵调那么好听，戏词儿也禁琢磨，演员的表演更是一举手一投足都那么讲究。现在我们一群票友经常聚在一起唱几句，那感觉别提多舒坦了。

[中国] 贺国强，男，退休职员

第一次看京剧我就被演员的服装和脸谱吸引住了，眼前舞动着这么多鲜艳的颜色真让人感叹。演员对每一个动作都能很好地把握，哪怕只是长袖震动或眼球旋转这样的小动作，演员也会十分优美而含着感情来完成。此外，我对京剧观众们的态度也感到很惊讶。边吃零食边看剧，听到特别悦耳的歌唱声就喊一声"好"，看到特别优秀的武功就热烈拍手。这种活泼热闹的气氛使我觉得，京剧和大众的关系很特别，很亲密。

[瑞士] 李斐，男，大学生

I loved to watch the noisy martial operas when I was young but began to watch operas characterized by singing and acting later. I am able to gain knowledge from the operas because many historical events appear in them. The images of the roles are quite obvious and one can distinguish the loyal ones from the evil ones easily. Since I am aged now, I love operas characterized by singing and acting more. The way of singing and the tone are quite pleasant to hear. The actors' lines are worth repeated consideration. Each gesture and expression in the performance is also elegant. Many amateur performers and I often get together to sing a few lines, which makes us quite comfortable.

[China] He Guoqiang, male, retiree

I was attracted by the actors' costume and facial make-up the first time I watched Beijing Opera. The rich colors before my eyes are quite amazing. The performers master every action. Even small ones such as shaking the long sleeve or moving the eyes are performed elegantly with emotions. Moreover, I also feel surprised by the audience who watch the opera while eating snacks, shout "good" when hearing pleasant singing, and applaud widely after seeing excellent martial art performance. The lively atmosphere makes me feel that the relationship between Beijing Opera and the general public is quite special and close.

[Switzerland] Li Fei, male, university student

小链接 ADDITIONAL INFORMATION

2010 年，一首《忐忑》在网上疯传，这首只有"嗯啊唉哟……"的歌由龚琳娜演唱，其夫老锣（Robert Zollitsch）作曲，唱词为戏曲锣鼓经，用笙、笛、提琴、扬琴等乐器伴奏，老旦、老生、黑头、花旦等多种音色在快速的节奏中变化无穷，独具新意。

In 2010, the song "Tan Te" spread across the Internet. It is sang by Gong Linna and composed by her husband Robert Zollitsch only with the sounds of "en, a, ai, you…" The lyrics are classics of gong and drum in operas and it is accompanied by musical instruments such as *sheng*, flute, violin and dulcimer. Voices of *laodan*, *laosheng*, *heitou* and *huadan* change endlessly in the fast rhythm, making the song quite new and unique.

龚琳娜和丈夫老锣
Gong Linna and her husband Robert Zollitsch

园 林
Chinese Gardens

　　在中国的名胜古迹中，颐和园的知名度不亚于故宫，它是到北京的中外游客必游之处。那气派非凡的万寿山、那波光粼粼的昆明湖、那形态各异的西堤六桥、那小巧玲珑的园中之园……行走在颐和园中，时时让你耳目一新，处处让你流连忘返。

In China's places of interest, the Summer Palace, as well-known as the Forbidden City, is a must for Chinese and foreign visitors in Beijing. The magnificent Longevity Hill, sparkling Kunming Lake, six bridges of various shapes on the West Causeway, and the small garden within the garden... Walking in the Summer Palace, you will find everything fresh and new and indulge yourself in pleasures without stopping.

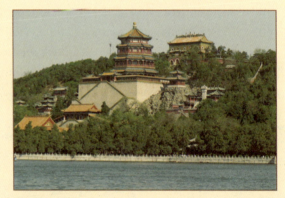

颐和园，田琨摄
The Summer Palace, photographed by Tian Kun

　　不同国家的园林各具特色，以中国园林与法国园林为例，差异就是显而易见的。中国园林要体现"天人合一"的观念，让山水、植物、建筑构成一个和谐的整体，既源于自然，又高于自然，正如明代造园家计成在《园冶》中所说："虽由人作，宛自天开。"法国园林重在表现人的力量，流行整

Gardens in different countries have their own features. For example, Chinese gardens and French gardens are obviously different from each other. Based on the theory that man is an integral part of nature, Chinese gardens harmoniously combine water, plants and buildings, which are derived from nature but above nature. As is said by Ji Cheng, a garden-designer in the Ming Dynasty, in

齐、对称的几何图形格局，通过人工美表现人对自然的控制与改造，有笔直的道路、规整的水池、华丽的雕像、壮美的建筑，以满足其举行盛大宴会或舞会的要求。

中国古典园林可分为皇家园林与私家园林。由于政治、经济、文化和自然地理条件的差异，皇家园林与私家园林在规模、布局、风格、色彩等方面均有明显差异，皇家园林以宏大、严整、艳丽著称，而私家园林以小巧、自由、淡雅见长。

颐和园是皇家园林的典范，位于北京西北郊，"乾隆十五年（1750）建为清漪园，后为庆其母60寿而起大报恩延寿寺于山，更山名为万寿，湖为昆明，乃初具规模。光绪十四年（1888）慈禧太后在此大肆兴构增筑，

Art of Garden-Building, "Although it is built by human beings, it seems to be created by God." French gardens, however, stress human power and feature the structure of symmetrical geometric figures. It shows humans' control and transformation of nature through artificial beauty, including straight roads, well-shaped pools, gorgeous sculptures and magnificent buildings to meet the needs of holding big dinner parties or dancing parties.

Chinese classical gardens include royal gardens and private gardens. Due to political, economic, cultural and geographic differences, royal gardens and private gardens differ greatly from each other in size, structure, style, and color with the former ones being famous for magnificence, neat formation and gorgeousness while the latter ones being loved for their exquisiteness, free design and elegance.

The Summer Palace, located on the northwestern outskirts of Beijing, is a model for royal gardens. "The Emperor Qianlong built Qingyi Garden during the 15th year of his reign. Later, to celebrate his mother's 60th birthday, he built the Temple of Gratitude

法国园林，刘谦功摄　　*French gardens, photographed by Liu Qiangong*

颐和园长廊，田琨摄
The long corridor in the Summer Palace, photographed by Tian Kun

经 22 年落成，并定名为颐和园。"①
颐和园北部以万寿山为中心，山腰有排云殿，山顶有佛香阁，山脚有长廊；南部以昆明湖为主体，水面开阔，龙王岛与万寿山巧成对景，以十七孔桥与东岸连接，西岸有形态各异的六座桥梁与一座景明楼。颐和园集中国造园艺术之大成，是中国古代园林艺术的卓越代表。

　　拙政园是私家园林的代表，唐代是文人陆龟蒙的居所，元代为大宏寺，明代御史王献臣改建成别业。园名"拙政"出自西晋文人潘岳的《闲居赋》："庶浮云之志，筑室种树，灌园鬻蔬……逍遥自得，此亦拙者之为政也。"拙政园以水景取胜，布局非常巧妙，利用山岛、洲渚、水流的聚合分割空

for Longevity on the hill and changed the name into Longevity Hill and Kunming Lake, therein the Summer Palace began to take shape. In the 14th year of the Emperor Guangxu's reign (1888), Empress Dowager Cixi began to construct a great number of buildings there, and completed them after 22 years, and named them collectively as the Summer Palace." ① The northern part of the Summer Palace is centered around Longevity Hill with the Hall of Dispelling Clouds on the hillside, the Tower of Buddhist Incense on the top and a long corridor at the foot. The southern part is mainly composed of the Kunming Lake with open water. The Dragon King Island is the scenery opposite of Longevity Hill and linked to the East Bank with the Seventeen-Arch Bridge. On the West Bank there are six bridges of various shapes and the Jingming Building. The Summer Palace is a comprehensive expression of Chinese garden-building arts and an outstanding representative of ancient Chinese garden art.

The Humble Administrator's Garden is representative of private gardens. It was the residence of the scholar Lu Guimeng in the Tang Dynasty, Dahong Temple in the Yuan Dynasty and it was rebuilt as a villa by Wang Xianchen, a messenger in the Ming Dynasty.

① 参见中央美术学院美术史系中国美术史教研室，《中国美术简史》（增订本），中国青年出版社，2002 年版，第 320 页。

① See also Teaching and Research Section of Chinese Art History of Art History Department in China Central Academy of the Arts. *A Brief History of Chinese Art*. Beijing: China Youth Press, 2002, page 320.

间，构成以远香堂为主的不同景区，各景区之间又借曲廊、小桥相互连接，处处诗情画意。

中国造园艺术在 18 世纪对欧洲有较大影响，其原因是"古典主义"[1]的衰落与"中国热"[2]的升温，影响到的国家主要有英国、法国、德国、荷兰等。例如，英国的斯道维花园（Stowe）始建于 1714 年，其平面图于 1739 年正式发表过，由此图可见，该园中除了有迂回盘绕的小径之外，树木也不修剪，还有中国式的叠石假山和山洞。时至今日，欧洲的一些园林中依然可见中国造园艺术的影响。

It derives its name from *Ode to a Quiet Life* by the scholar Pan Yue in the Western Jin Dynasty. "Perhaps the modest ambition is to build the house, plant the tree, water the garden and cultivate the vegetables...I feel free and unfettered and this is a suitable way for humble people to live." The Humble Administrator's Garden is well-known for the waterscape. Being well structured, it divides space by hills, land on the water and the confluence of flowing water, and forms different scenic spots with the Yuanxiang Hall as the main attraction. The scenic spots are linked with each other by zigzag verandas and small bridges, thus making everywhere appear poetic and picturesque.

The garden-building art in China has a great influence on European countries such as England, France, Germany, and Netherlands in 18th century because of the decline of classicism [1] and the rise of "Sinomania" [2] . For example, the Stowe Garden in Great Britain was originally built in 1714. Its plan, officially published in 1739, shows that it has winding trails, unpruned trees, and Chinese-style rockery artificial hills and caves. Even to this day, some European gardens are still influenced by Chinese garden-building art.

拙政园，李佳琳摄
The Humble Administrator's Garden, photographed by Li Jialin

[1] 古典主义：17 世纪流行于西欧特别是法国的一种思潮，以古希腊、罗马文学艺术为样板，至 19 世纪浪漫主义兴起而结束。

[2] 中国热：指 18 世纪流行于欧洲的中国风尚，渗透到欧洲人生活的各个层面，如日用物品、家居装饰、园林建筑等。

[1] Classicism: an ideological trend with ancient Greek and Roman literature and art as prototypes prevailing in Western Europe, especially France from the 17th century to the 19th century when romanticism prevailed.

[2] Sinomania: the Chinese fashion which was popular in Europe in the 18th century and extended into many aspects of life including daily necessities, home decorations and garden buildings.

三言两语 A FEW REMARKS

中国园林，名之为"文人园"。它是饶有书卷气的园林艺术。因为建筑与园林结合得好，人们称之为"有书卷气的高雅建筑"，我则首先誉之为"雅洁明净，得清新之致"，两者意思是相同的，足证历代谈中国园林总离不了中国诗文。所谓"诗中有画，画中有诗"，归根到底脱不开诗文一事。这就是中国造园的主导思想。

[中国] 陈从周，男，古建筑学家

园林在中国的传统艺术中占有重要的地位，园林设计的艺术可以追溯到公元前 3000 年。第一次进入一个中国园林时我感到很吃惊，因为我一听园林就会想到树林、花朵、绿草等植物，但中国的园林却不同，它们是以各种形状的假山、小湖、小丘为主。园林的样子是精确地设计出来的，但却没失去自然的味道。有一种跟外界完全隔离的感觉，就像进入了一个完美的小世界一样。

[奥地利] 齐傲华，女，大学生

Chinese garden, also known as the "scholar garden", is a kind of garden art with a scholar's flavoring. Due to its good combination of architecture and gardens, people call it "elegant architecture of a scholar's style" and I praise it as "decent, bright, clean, pure and fresh", which is the same meaning as the former one. These are enough to prove that Chinese gardens in all ages are associated with poems and prose. The concept of "painting-in-poetry and poetry-in-painting" means that paintings and poetry are essentially linked to each other and this is the dominant idea in Chinese garden-building.

[China] Chen Congzhou, male, expert on ancient architecture

Gardens play an important role in Chinese traditional arts. Garden-design art can be dated back to 3000 BC. I felt surprised when I first stepped into a Chinese garden because I would think of plants like trees, flowers and green grass at the mention of a garden. However, Chinese gardens are different and mainly contain rockeries, lakes and hills of various shapes. The gardens are carefully designed but preserve the features of nature. They make me feel totally isolated from the outside world and I feel I am entering a small but perfect realm.

[Austria] Qi Aohua, female, university student

小链接 ADDITIONAL INFORMATION

　　蒙梭花园（Monceau）是一座颇具中国园林风格的法国园林，始建于 1773 年，风景如画，水面宽阔且富于变化，包括湖泊、小溪和跌水①。该花园以水面为中心，湖心有一个小岛，岛上有中国式建筑物以及中国园林常设的小桥、岩洞和假山。该花园疏朗的布局、蜿蜒的小径、随意摆放的雕像均有别于严谨、对称、精心打理的传统法式花园。

莫奈《蒙梭花园》，1878 年
Monceau Park, Monet, 1878

The Monceau Park is a French garden with Chinese garden characteristics. Originally built in 1773, it is picturesque with wide and changing water including lakes, streams and water fall ① .

The garden is centered around the water. In the middle of the lake lays an island on which there are Chinese-style buildings, bridges, rock caves and rockeries that often appear in Chinese gardens. The clear structure, winding trails and randomly placed sculptures are different from those of the traditional French gardens which are rigorous, symmetrical, and carefully taken care of.

① 跌水：底部为阶梯形、呈瀑布跌落状的水流，有天然跌水和人工跌水之分，后者常用于园林水景设计。

① Water fall: water flow dropping like waterfalls with the bottom shaped like stairs. It includes natural water falls and artificial water falls and the man-made one is often used in garden waterscape designs.

Chinese Culture
Symbols

文化符号

文房四宝
Four Treasures of Study

导入 INTRODUCTION

在 2008 年北京奥运会开幕式上，一轴长卷渐渐展开，舞蹈演员们用自己独特的身体语言，将中国"文房四宝"——笔、墨、纸、砚所创造的神奇画卷展示在世人面前——那就是北宋王希孟所绘的意境壮美、气势恢宏的《千里江山图》。

In the opening ceremony of the Beijing Olympic Games in 2008, a scroll gradually unfolded and the dancers, using their unique body language, presented before the whole world a magical picture scroll created by writing brushes, ink sticks, paper and ink stones, the Four Treasures of Study in China. The scroll is the magnificent and beautiful *Picture of the Landscape of a Thousand Miles* drawn by Wang Ximeng in the Northern Song Dynasty.

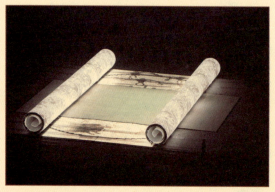

2008 年北京奥运会开幕式上的中国画卷
The Chinese picture scroll in the opening ceremony of the Beijing Olympic Games in 2008

自古以来，中国人一直有崇尚读书的传统，尤其把书法和绘画作为评判一个人文化素养的标准，就连皇帝也是如此，宋徽宗的绘画、清乾隆的书法都很著名。要读书就要有书房，书房也叫文房，笔、墨、纸、砚是书房必备之物，故称之为"文房四宝"。文房四宝各有精品，其中湖笔、徽墨、宣纸、端砚最为著名。

Since ancient times, Chinese people advocated reading and even judged one's cultural literacy by calligraphy and painting. Even the emperors think so and the paintings of Emperor Huizong of the Song Dynasty and the calligraphy of Emperor Qianlong of the Qing Dynasty are quite well-known. Reading books requires studies and writing brushes, ink sticks, paper and ink stones are called the Four Treasures of Study because they are

湖笔
The writing brush produced in Huzhou

　　笔指毛笔，产生于新石器时代，彩陶上的图画就是用毛笔描绘的。毛笔主要是用动物的毛制成的，羊毛制的叫"羊毫"、黄鼠狼的尾毛制的叫"狼毫"。今天虽然流行铅笔、钢笔、圆珠笔，甚至可以用电脑写字画画儿，却都替代不了毛笔，因为用毛笔写字绘画那种独特的艺术效果是任何种类的笔都模仿不来的。

　　墨是书写、绘画用的色料，有不同的产地、不同的品种，徽墨是其中的精品。这里面有一个故事：五代十国时期由制墨名匠奚超、奚廷圭父子研制出一种好墨，深受南唐后主李煜的赏识，全家赐国姓"李氏"，从此"李墨"名满天下，宋时李墨的产地歙县改名徽州，"李墨"因之也改名为"徽墨"。

indispensible in the studies. Among the high-quality treasures, the writing brush produced in Huzhou, the ink stick produced in Huizhou, the *xuan* paper made in Xuancheng and the inkstone made in Duanxi are the most renowned.

The writing brushes were produced in the Neolithic Age and can be used to draw the pictures on painted potteries. They are mainly made of the hair of animals. Those made of wool are called *yanghao* and those made of the hair with the tail of weasel are called *langhao*. Today's popular pencils, pens, ballpoint pens and even computers which are able to write and paint cannot replace writing brushes whose unique artistic effects in writing and painting cannot be imitated by any other pens.

The ink stick is the pigment used in writing and painting and it is produced in different places with various kinds. The ink stick produced in Huizhou is of high quality. A story goes like this: Xi Chao and his son Xi Tinggui, two craftsmen famous for making

徽墨
The ink stick produced in Huizhou

纸是中国的四大发明之一，汉代（前206—公元220）开始制造，蔡伦在很大程度上改良了工艺，隋唐（581—907）时期著名的宣纸诞生。在宣纸的产地安徽宣州有这样一个传说：蔡伦的徒弟孔丹以造纸为业，一直想造一种理想的白纸，但多次试验都没有成功。后来他在山里偶然看到倒在山涧旁的檀树被水浸得发白，便用这种树皮造出了宣纸。宣纸质地柔韧、色泽洁白、吸水力强、平滑感好，在国际上享有"纸寿千年"的美誉。

砚是书写、绘画时研磨色料的工具，汉代（前206—公元220）已流行，明清两代（1368—1911）品种繁多，

宣纸
Xuan paper

ink sticks in the Southern Tang Dynasty in the Five Dynasties and Ten Kingdoms Period, were greatly appreciated by the Emperor Li Yu in the Southern Tang Dynasty who granted their whole family the surname "Li" because they produced a kind of high-quality ink stick. From then on, the fame of the Li Ink Stick was widespread. In the Song Dynasty, after the name of Shexian, the producing area of Li Ink Stick, was changed into Huizhou, and the Li Ink Stick was then referred to as the Hui Ink Stick (the ink stick produced in Huizhou).

Paper is among the four great inventions in ancient China. It was first made in the Han Dynasty (206 BC-AD 220) and then it was greatly refined by Cai Lun. The famous *xuan* paper came into existence in the Sui and Tang dynasties (581-907). In Xuanzhou, Anhui Province where the *xuan* paper is produced, it is said that Cai Lun's apprentice Kong Dan took the job of producing paper but failed in his attempts in making ideal white paper. Later he happened to see that the ebony falling on the mountain stream was soaked by the water and turned white. Then he used the bark to produce *xuan* paper which is reputed worldwide as "paper that can last for one thousand years" due to its flexible texture, white color, good water-absorbing quality and smoothness.

As the tool used for grinding the pigment in writing and painting, ink stone was already very popular in the Han Dynasty (206 BC-AD 220). The Ming and Qing dynasties (1368-1911) witnessed the great variety of ink stones as well as the appearance of the Four Famous

出现了被称为"四大名砚"的端砚、歙砚、洮砚、澄泥砚。这些砚台工艺精湛、造型美观，不写不画也可用来观赏。

端砚　　*Duan Ink Stone*

Ink Stones—Duan Ink Stone, She Ink Stone, Tao Ink Stone and Chengni Ink Stone. They can not only be used in writing and painting but also for admiration due to their exquisite workmanship and attractive appearance.

"文房四宝"不仅是有实用价值的文具，同时也是集绘画、书法、雕刻为一体的艺术品。北京故宫博物院收藏了许多珍贵的文房四宝，是皇家御用之物，用料考究，工艺精美，代表了中国历史上数千年来文房用具发展的最高水平。

The Four Treasures of Study are not only stationery with use value but also works of art combining painting, calligraphy and carving. The Palace Museum in Beijing has collected many precious and imperial Four Treasures of Study made with selected materials and exquisite workmanship, representing the highest quality of stationery during the thousands of years in Chinese history.

三言两语 A FEW REMARKS

我认为笔、墨、纸、砚于中国传统文人而言，缺一不可。要在中国传统文人中间找到一条一致认同的共通性，恐怕也只有这与之长相厮守的"文房四宝"堪任其职了。而作为书法和绘画的工具，传统的笔墨纸砚还在使用，使我们得以熏陶于独特的艺术韵味之中。另一方面，其本身的取材和制作之精细讲究暂且不论，就其形制而言，在满足了各种实用要求后，早已由实用而艺术了。

[中国]杨白水，男，大学教授

我是泰国留学生，选修过中国书法课，第一次上课老师就给我们讲了"文房四宝"，主要是笔、墨、纸、砚的来源和作用。我觉得中国人真棒，他们能创造出这么有意思的文具，而

In my opinion, writing brushes, ink sticks, paper and ink stones are all indispensible for Chinese scholars. Perhaps the only thing shared and recognized by all traditional Chinese scholars is the Four Treasures of Study which have accompanied them for such a long time. The traditional writing brushes, ink sticks, paper and ink stones are still in use as the tools for calligraphy and painting, so that we can still be nurtured by this special and charming art. On the other hand, apart from the carefully selected materials and sophisticated production, the shapes and structures of them can not only meet various practical needs but also offer artistic appeal.

[China] Yang Baishui, male, university professor

As a foreign student from Thailand, I once selected the course of Chinese calligraphy.

且还让这些东西保留到今天，使我有机会了解到它，我为中国人感到骄傲。虽然我很久没有写书法了，可是这些知识还留在我的记忆中，希望将来有更多的人有机会了解到它。

[泰国] 陈明月，男，大学生

In the first class, the teacher introduced to us the Four Treasures of Study and mainly talked about the origins and functions of writing brushes, ink sticks, paper and ink stones. I think that Chinese people are so great because they invented the interesting stationery and have kept them till today so that I have the opportunity to know about them. I am very proud of Chinese people. Although I have not practiced calligraphy for a long time, the knowledge is still in my mind and I hope that more people will have the opportunity to know it in the future.

[Thailand] Chen Mingyue, male, university student

小链接 ADDITIONAL INFORMATION

中国的水墨画与欧洲的油画在艺术效果与绘画风格上大相径庭，这与其使用的工具不同有很大关系。中国画使用"文房四宝"笔、墨、纸、砚，而西洋画的工具主要有画笔、画刀、画布、调色板、油壶、洗笔器。画笔用于调色和画面着色；画刀可以刮色和清理画板；画布以厚实均匀、无结点和孔隙的亚麻织品为最佳；调色板用于调色及摆置颜料；油壶盛装调色油、松节油等调和剂；洗笔器是用来洗刷或搁置带颜料的画笔的。

荷兰画家伦勃朗的《夜巡》（阿姆斯特丹国立美术馆藏）
The Night Watch by Dutch painter Rembrandt (reserved in the Rijksmuseum)

Chinese wash paintings vary greatly from Western oil paintings in artistic effect and painting style largely because of their different tools. Chinese paintings use writing brushes, ink sticks, paper and ink stones while Western paintings use painting brushes, painting knives, canvas, color palettes, oilers, and brush-washing machines. Painting brushes are used to mix the colors and put colors on the painting; painting knives are used to scrape the color and clean up the drawing board; the best canvas is made of thick and homogenous linens without knots or holes; color palettes are used to mix the colors and put the pigment; oilers are used to hold blenders such as megilp and turpentine; brush-washing machines are used to wash or put painting brushes with pigment on them.

汉 字
Chinese Characters

导入 INTRODUCTION

2008 年，第 29 届奥运会在北京举办，会徽"舞动的北京"上半部分是一个像人形的"京"字中国印，镌刻着一个拥有十三亿人口和五十六个民族的国家对奥林匹克运动的誓言，充分体现了汉字的魅力。

In the 29th Beijing Olympic Games in 2008, the upper part of the emblem *Dancing Beijing* is a human-shaped Chinese seal—*jing*(京), embodying the Olympic Oath of a country with 1.3 billion and 56 ethnic groups and fully reflecting the charm of Chinese characters.

北京奥运会会徽（张武、郭春宁、毛诚设计）

The emblem of the Beijing Olympic Games (designed by Zhang Wu, Guo Chunning and Mao Cheng)

汉字是记录汉语的符号，起源于象形。中国古代先民通过刻画图像等方法创造了汉字，在此基础上又采用更多的方法创制出数万个汉字。清康熙五十五年（1716）的《康熙字典》[1] 收录了 47035 个汉字，1994 年的《中华字海》收录了 85568 个汉字。

关于汉字的造字方法和使用方法，东汉（25—220）的许慎在《说文解字》中进行了总结，即著名的"六书"——象形、指事、会意、形声、

As the signs to record the Chinese language, Chinese characters originated from pictographs. Ancient Chinese people created Chinese characters by means of depicting the images and on this basis invented thousands of characters with more methods. The *Kangxi Dictionary* [1] in the 55th year of the reign of Emperor Kangxi includes 47,035 Chinese characters and the *Sea of Chinese Characters* in 1994 includes 85,568 Chinese characters.

In the Eastern Han Dynasty (25-220), Xu Shen summarized in *An Analytical Dictionary*

---

[1] 《康熙字典》由张玉书、陈廷敬主持编纂，成书于 1716 年。字典采用部首分类法，按笔画排列单字，共分为十二集，以十二地支标识，每集又分为上、中、下三卷，并按韵母、声调以及音节分类排列韵母表及其对应汉字，共收录汉字 47035 个。

[1] *Kangxi Dictionary* was compiled by Zhang Yushu and Chen Tingjing and finished in 1716. The dictionary classifies Chinese words by radicals and arranges the individual characters based on their strokes. It includes 12 units, each of which is marked by the Twelve Earthly Branches and divided into three volumes, and classifies and arranges the vowel list and the corresponding Chinese characters according to the vowels, tones and syllables.

转注、假借。"转注、假借"是用字方法，前面的"四书"才是真正的造字方法，包含着深刻的内涵和有趣的故事。

甲骨文"鱼"字
"鱼" (fish) in Oracle

金文"电"字
"电" (electricity) in Chinese bronze inscriptions

　　所谓"象形"，即汉字本身就是描摹事物的形状的。例如，"鱼"字上面是头，中间是身子，下面是尾巴。象形字来源于图画，但在演变过程中图画性质逐渐减弱，象征性质逐渐增强，例如，"电"是象形字，描摹闪电划过天空的情形，因为它总是在下雨时出现，金文还给它加了个雨字头——"電"。"闪电的速度很快，人们常用它来形容行动迅速。秦始皇有七匹名马，其中一匹叫做'追电'，是说这匹骏马跑得很快，快到能追上闪电了。西汉的汉文帝也有骏马九匹，其中一匹是赤红色的，跑起来像一道赤色的闪电，名叫'赤电'。"① 中国人看到象形字，相应的画面便会出现在脑海中。

of Characters the word-formation and application methods, which are the famous six categories of Chinese characters— pictographs, selfexplanatory characters, associative compounds, pictophonetic characters, mutually explanatory characters and loan characters. The latter two are application methods while the former four are real word-formation methods which embody deep meanings and interesting stories.

As being a kind of pictographs, this means that Chinese characters describe the shapes of things. For example, the upper part of "鱼" (fish) is the head, the middle part is the body and the bottom part is the tail. Pictographs originated from pictures and gradually became more symbolic with less picture characteristics. For instance, "电" (electricity) is a pictograph describing the lightning flashing across the sky. Since it always appears in the rain, Chinese bronze inscriptions add a "雨" (rain) to it and turn it into "電". "People always use the lightning to describe the rapid action because of its fast speed. The First Emperor of the Qin Dynasty had seven horses, one of which was called 'catching up with the lightning', implying that the horse runs so fast that it can catch up with the lightning. The Emperor Wen of the Western Han Dynasty also had nine horses, amongst which a red one ran like lightning and was called 'red lightning'."[1] At the sight of pictographs, Chinese people will think about the corresponding pictures.

Self-explanatory characters mean forming characters with symbolic signs. For instance,

---

① 参见任犀然，《汉字中华》，当代世界出版社，2010年版，第39页。

[1] See *A Canon of Chinese Characters* by Ren Xiran, The Contemporary World Press, 2010, page 39.

闪电，田琨摄
Lightning, photographed by Tian Kun

所谓指事，即用象征性的符号构成汉字。例如，"刃"字是在刀锋处加上一点；"上、下"二字表示在主体"一"的上方和下方；而"本、末"二字表示树根和树梢。与象形字相比，这些字的某个部分在造字时就是抽象的。

所谓会意，即汉字整体的意义是由部分的意义合成的。例如，"酒"字将酿酒的瓦罐"酉"和液体"水"合起来表达字义；"信"字将"人"和"言"合起来表示人说话有信用。字典在解释会意字时，常常用"从……从……"的格式，例如："鸣"

"刃" (knife-edge) is to add a point to the edge of the "刀" (knife); "上" (above) and "下" (below) means to be above or below the main body " 一 "; " 本 " and " 末 " refer to tree root and treetop. Compared with pictographs, certain parts of these characters were abstract in word-formation.

Associative compounds indicate that the meaning of the whole character is the combination of the meanings of different parts. For example, "酒" (wine) expresses its meaning by combining the crock used to brew wine "酉" with the liquid "水"; "信" combines "人" (human) with "言" (word) to imply that people keep their words. While explaining associative compounds, dictionaries always use the form of "从……从……". For example, "鸣" 从口从鸟，会鸟叫之意.["鸣" combines "口" (mouth) with "鸟" (bird) and means the sound of bird].

Pictophonetic characters refer to characters formed on the basis of images and pronunciations. The radical part is related to the meaning of the character and the phonetic part is related to the pronunciation. For

鸣，田琨摄
The sound of bird, photographed by Tian Kun

书法是汉字的艺术——苏东坡的《黄州寒食帖》（中国台北"故宫博物院"藏）
Calligraphy is the art of Chinese characters—Huang Zhou Han Shi Tie by Su Shi (reserved in Taipei Palace Museum, China)

从口从鸟，会鸟叫之意。

所谓形声，即汉字由形和声两部分合成，形旁和全字的意义有关，声旁和全字的读音有关。例如，"榕"字左边表形，右边表声；"齿"字下边表形，上边表声；"围"字外边表形，里边表声。由于"形声"具有强大的造字功能，所以东汉的《说文解字》中就有 80% 以上的汉字是用这种方法构成的。

有一首流行歌曲《中国娃》[①]唱道："最爱说的话呀永远是中国话，字正腔圆落地有声说话最算话；最爱写的字是先生教的方块字，横平竖直堂堂正正做人也像它。"汉字有着丰富的文化内涵和象征意义，引发人们真善美的感受。

instance, the left part of "榕" refers to its image and the right part indicates its pronunciation. The upper part of "齿" shows its pronunciation and the bottom part shows its image. The outer part of "围" indicates its shape and the inner part indicates its pronunciation. Due to the powerful functions of pictophonetic characters, over 80% of characters in *An Analytical Dictionary of Characters* in the Eastern Han Dynasty were created in this way.

The popular song "Chinese Youths"[①] goes like this, "My favorite language is always Chinese with clear articulation and a mellow and full tune. People who speak the language are most trustworthy. My favorite written words are Chinese characters with straight horizontal and vertical strokes taught by the teachers. People should also be upright like the Chinese characters." Chinese characters embody rich cultural connotation and symbolic meaning and trigger feelings of the true, the good and the beautiful from people's hearts.

[①] 《中国娃》由曲波作词、戚建波作曲，在 1997 年春节晚会上由解晓东演唱。

[①] composed by Qi Jianbo, lyrics written by Qu Bo, sang by Xie Xiaodong in Spring Festival Gala in 1997.

三言两语 A FEW REMARKS

汉字是世界上最古老的文字之一，在形体上逐渐由图形变为由笔画构成的方块形符号，所以汉字一般也叫"方块字"。汉字具有集形象、声音和辞义三者于一体的特性。这一特性在世界文字中是独一无二的，汉字是中华民族几千年文化的瑰宝。

[中国] 郝晓刚，男，企业经理

刚来中国时我觉得汉字像天书一般，看不懂也记不住。开始老师让我们背一些汉字，但在我的国家我们很少背东西，我想我一定能找出学习汉字的一种新办法来。过了一年的时间，我一直没有掌握学汉字的要领，后来我终于放弃了，要想学好汉字，只能按中国人的办法来学。我以为我永远学不会汉字，因为汉字看起来特难，特复杂，而现在，我知道只要努力，只要坚持下去，就没有什么不可能的事。

[巴西] 德比，女，大学生

Chinese characters are one of the most ancient character sets in the world. They are also called "Square Characters" for they are square signs with strokes transformed from images. Chinese characters combine images, pronunciations and meanings, which is a unique thing in the world. Chinese characters are a gem of the Chinese nation's several thousand years of culture.

[China] Hao Xiaogang, male, company manager

When I just arrived in China, I thought Chinese characters were so difficult that I could neither understand nor memorize them. At the beginning, the teacher asked us to memorize some Chinese characters. However, I seldom memorized things in my country, so I thought that I would certainly find a new way to learn Chinese characters. One year later, I still failed to grasp the way to learn Chinese characters. Finally I gave it up and realized that I could only learn Chinese characters in Chinese people's way. I thought that I would never master Chinese characters because they look so difficult and sophisticated. At present, however, I am aware that nothing is impossible with great efforts and persistence.

[Brazil] Derby, female, university student

小链接 ADDITIONAL INFORMATION

字谜是一种文字游戏，方块汉字具有笔画纷繁复杂、偏旁相对独立、结构灵活多变等特点，因而可以运用离合、增损、象形、会意等多种方式进行猜测汉字的游戏。字谜既可以益智又非常有趣，从古至今一直深受人们喜爱。请看下面这些字谜：

少女——妙　　　　　　　　一加一——王

一个人——大　　　　　　　文武双全——斌

人不在其位——立　　　　　大雨落在横山上——雪

千里姻缘一线牵——重　　　一边绿，一边红；绿的喜雨，红的喜风——秋

Riddle about characters is a word game. Since Chinese characters have numerous and complicated strokes, relatively independent radicals, and flexible structures, Chinese characters can be guessed through separation and reunion, loss and gain, describing the shapes of things and combining different elements of the characters. Being both educational and interesting, the riddles have been deeply loved by people in all ages. Please take a look at the following riddles about Chinese characters.

少女 (young girl) —— 妙

一加一 (one plus one) —— 王

一个人 (one person) —— 大

文武双全 (be adept with both the pen and the sword) —— 斌

人不在其位 (people not in their position) —— 立

大雨落在横山上 (rain falling on the mountain) —— 雪

千里姻缘一线牵 (A fate match across a thousand miles is drawn by a thread.) —— 重

一边绿，一边红；绿的喜雨，红的喜风 (One side is green and the other is red; the green one prefers rain while the red one prefers wind.) —— 秋

Tourism Highlights

名胜 古迹

兵马俑

Terracotta Warriors

导入 INTRODUCTION

秦始皇陵一号铜车马（秦始皇陵兵马俑博物馆藏）

The No.1 Bronze Chariot and Horses of Emperor Qin Shihuang's Mausoleum (reserved in Emperor Qin Shihuang's Mausoleum Site Museum)

2010 年上海世博会上，中国国家馆展出了国宝"秦始皇陵一号铜车马"，双轮、单辕、驷马系驾，总重量约 1040 公斤，有一千多件金银配饰，通体彩绘。这件铜车马为秦始皇陵兵马俑博物馆所藏，它背后有一个庞大无比、精湛绝伦的战阵——秦始皇陵兵马俑。

During Expo 2010 Shanghai China, the national treasure No.1 Bronze Chariot and Horses of Emperor Qin Shihuang's Mausoleum, a two-wheeled vehicle with one shaft, drawn by a team of four horses, with a total weight of 1,040 kilograms, bearing more than one thousand pieces of bullion and painted all over with colorful patterns was exhibited in the China Pavilion. At the back of the bronze chariot and horses, one of the collections of Emperor Qin Shihuang's Mausoleum Site Museum, lies an immense and splendid battle array—the Terracotta Warriors.

秦始皇是中国封建社会大一统帝国的始皇帝，是秦人乃至秦朝的杰出代表。秦人质朴、尚武，他们来自黄土飞扬的八百里秦川，信奉"制天命而用之"的法家思想，他们的艺术亦如其人那样浑厚且阳刚，最具代表性的，莫过于秦始皇陵兵马俑了。

秦始皇陵有着巨大的陵体，其地下世界极其恢宏，20 世纪 70 年代

Qin Shihuang, the first emperor who unified feudal China, is an outstanding representative of the people of Qin or even the Qin Dynasty. The rustic people of Qin honored martial arts and inhabited the Guanzhong Plain of Shaanxi Province which is abundant in loess. They embraced the Legalist ideology of "adapting the law of heaven and making use of it". The art of these people precisely resembles their character—profound, vigorous and masculine, the most representative of

兵马俑，刘谦功摄
The Terracotta Warriors, photographed by Liu Qiangong

挖掘出来的阵容强大的秦始皇陵兵马俑充分证明了这一点，也充分展示了秦始皇统帅的、使中国归于一统的秦国军队的赫赫声威。

秦始皇陵兵马俑主要出土于1974年发现的一号坑和1976年发现的二、三号坑，三个坑内共有陶俑、陶马约8000件。一号坑以步兵为主，战车与步兵相间排列为长方形军阵；二号坑是车兵、骑兵、步兵混合排列的曲形阵；三号坑是军阵统帅的指挥部，古代称军幕。俑的种类繁多，因职位、兵种不同而装束、姿态各异，但都威武雄壮，而其组成的军阵规模之宏大、场面之壮观实属古今中外之罕见，充分体现出"秦王扫六合"①，"带甲百万，车千乘，骑万匹"②的磅礴气势。兵俑的高度一般在1.75—1.85米之间，有的身披铠甲，有的腰

which being nothing more than the Terracotta Warriors.

Emperor Qin Shihuang's Mausoleum has an impressive size of construction, whose underground vault is extraordinarily extensive. This fact is sufficiently attested by the magnificent formation of Terracotta Warriors excavated in the 1970s, which also fully exhibits the formidable prestige of the Qin army that unified China under the command of Qin Shihuang.

The Terracotta Warriors were mainly excavated from Pit No.1 discovered in 1974 and Pit No.2 and No.3 found in 1976. Altogether, the three pits housed approximately 8,000 Terracotta Warriors and horses. Pit No.1 consists mainly of infantrymen alternating with war chariots, forming a rectangular battle array; Pit No.2 is a curve, composite formation of chariot soldiers, cavalrymen and infantrymen; Pit No.3 is the headquarters of military commanders, which was referred to as "army tent" in ancient times. The Terracotta Warriors are of various types: their costumes and postures vary according to their different ranks and branches in the army; however, they are invariably mighty and magnificent. The extensive battle array and breathtaking scene are rarely found at all times and in all lands, which adequately displays the tremendous momentum of "Emperor Qin Shihuang annexing the six states" [1] by

① 语出西汉史学家司马迁的著作《史记》。
② 语出西汉经学家刘向校订的史书《战国策》。

[1] quoted from *Records of the Historian* by Sima Qian, a historian of the Western Han Dynasty.

佩长剑，有的手持长矛，表现出秦朝军人威武雄壮、英勇善战的军容，仿佛当初秦始皇"鞭笞天下、威震四海"① 靠的就是他们。马俑的高度一般为1.5米，体长2米，膘肥体壮，生气勃勃，表现出一种静则如山、动则如风的气势。

有一本《中国雕塑史》写道："如此之多的写实雕塑何以能如霹雳般出现于关中大地，我们也许更多地要从那种将秦人统一于一种精神状态的法家思想和秦人的某些族群性格来探究原因。……秦俑那朴素威武的神态，那重于写实的衣着，那整齐划一的阵势无处不体现着法家那种实用至上的思想光辉。在这种指导思想下，再加

三号坑——军幕，刘谦功摄
Pit No.3, the Army Tent, photographed by Liu Qiangong

"leading millions of soldiers, thousands of war chariots and tens of thousands of horses".① The Terracotta Warriors measure between 1.75-1.85 meters high, and some are wearing suits of armor, some armed with swords while others holding spears, giving off an impression of the powerfulness, bravery and skillfulness of the Qin army. It seems as if Emperor Qin Shihuang actually relied on these warriors to "prevail over the whole China and strike the world with awe".② The Terracotta Horses measuring in general 1.5 meters tall and 2 meters long are plump, robust and full of vitality; they manifest an imposing manner of as steady as the mountain when static, while swift as the wind when moving.

As is written in the book *A History of Chinese Sculpture,* "Why so many realistic sculptures appeared in Guanzhong Plain in a flash? We may gain an insight into the reason by exploring more from the Legalist thoughts that bound the people of Qin together in a unified mental state, as well as by exploring certain ethnic traits shared by these people. ...The simple yet mighty bearings of the Terracotta Warriors, the costumes emphasizing realistic representations, and the absolutely uniform battle array display in every detail the brilliance of practicality-oriented Legalist ideas. Considering this guiding principle as well as the rustic and profound ethnic traits of Qin people spontaneously developed in their life of cultivation and pasturing on the Loess Plateau, the discrepancy between the highly realistic nature of Terracotta Warriors and the

---

① 语出西汉政论家贾谊的文章《过秦论》。

① quoted from *Intrigues of the Warring States*, proofread and edited by Liu Xiang, a scripture compiler of the Western Han Dynasty.

② quoted from "Sins of Qin" by Jia Yi, a political commentator of the Western Han Dynasty.

上地处黄土高原的秦人在农耕和放牧生活中自发形成的朴实和厚重性格，兵马俑的高度写实与同时期的雕塑风格相比就不显得突兀而更容

雄壮的战阵，刘谦功摄
The magnificent battle array, photographed by Liu Qiangong

易理解了，甚至可以被看作是一种必然。"①秦始皇陵兵马俑是"威武之师"、"雄壮之师"，写的是力量之实，塑的是从容之态，是典型的秦风之作，充分表现出秦始皇开疆拓土、把中国推向大一统时代的气概。

contemporaneous sculptural style seems no longer abrupt but readily understandable, or can even be viewed as a kind of inevitability."① The Terracotta Warriors of Qin Shihuang's Mausoleum are a mighty army as well as a majestic troop; they depict the reality of military strength, model a state of calmness and represent a typical oeuvre of Qin's art; they sufficiently demonstrate Qin Shihuang's heroic mettle as he expanded the territory and pushed forward the unification of ancient China.

三言两语 A FEW REMARKS

秦始皇陵兵马俑制作得极其精美，一个个俑看似区别不大，实则迥异，而且他们所穿的铠甲皆有表明等级的标志，然而他们却有一点是相同的——都是单眼皮，据说因为秦始皇是单眼皮。秦始皇的神威由此可见一斑。

[中国]林志鹏，男，国家公务员

我喜欢舞刀弄枪，所以爸爸妈妈带我去西安旅行的时候，我看到兵马俑特别兴奋。听导游说一号坑出土的一把青铜剑被陶俑压住弯曲了两千多年，搬开陶俑后立即恢复了平直，

The Terracotta Warriors are made extremely exquisitely. They seem to have little difference with each other, but are actually quite distinct: their suits of armor invariably indicate their ranks. Nevertheless, they share one point in common—all of them have single-edged eyelids which reportedly resulted from Emperor Qin Shihuang's having of single-edged eyelid. So we can see Emperor Qin Shihuang's divinity is evident.

[China] Lin Zhipeng, male, civil servant

As I like brandishing swords and spears, so when my parents took me to travel in Xi'an, I was especially excited when I saw the

---

① 参见华梅主编，王家斌、王鹤著，《中国雕塑史》，天津人民出版社，2005年版，第48–49页。

① See also Wang Jiabin, Wang He, *A History of Chinese Sculpture*, Hua Mei ed. Tianjin: Tianjin People's Press, 2005, page 48-49.

实在是太神奇了！

[中国] 张勇，男，小学生

我去西安看过兵马俑，兵马俑的壮美难以用语言来形容。一个个健壮的士兵气定神闲，安静地看着前方，活灵活现，似乎随时都会复活过来，好壮观、好宏伟！这让我回想起一些历史事实，感受到中国皇帝具有的权力感。

[阿塞拜疆] 莱拉，女，大学生

Terracotta Warriors. I heard something from the tourist guide, saying that a bronze sword unearthed from Pit No.1, which was bent for more than two thousand years under the weight of Terracotta Warriors immediately restored its straightness once the warriors were removed. This is so marvelous!
[China] Zhang Yong, male, primary school student

I've been to Xi'an to visit the Terracotta Warriors whose splendor can hardly be described in words. The robust warriors are at leisure, looking forward with calmness; they are lifelike and seem to be coming alive at any moment. This reminded me of some historical events and enabled me to feel a sense of power possessed by Chinese emperors.
[Republic of Azerbaijan] Lara, female, college student

小链接 ADDITIONAL INFORMATION

埃及的狮身人面像与秦始皇陵兵马俑同样有名，据说它是奉胡夫的圣旨雕出来的：公元前 2610 年，法老胡夫来这里巡视自己快要竣工的陵墓金字塔，发现采石场上还有一块巨石，胡夫当即命令石匠们按照他的脸型雕一座狮身人面像。像雕成后高 20 米，长 57 米，头戴皇冠，额上刻着"库伯拉"（即 cobra，意思是眼镜蛇），下颌有帝王的标志——下垂的长须。如果你想象不出这座雕像到底有多大，那我可以告诉你一个具体的数据——他的耳朵有两米多长。

埃及金字塔前的狮身人面像
The Great Sphinx of Giza in Egypt, in front of the Pyramid

The Great Sphinx of Giza in Egypt enjoys equal reputation as the Terracotta Warriors. It is said that, the Sphinx was carved upon the imperial edict issued by Khufu: in the year 2610 BC, when pharaoh Khufu was on a tour of inspection at the site of his own pyramid which was near completion, he found in the quarry a huge piece of stone. He immediately ordered the stonemasons to carve a sphinx according to the outlines of his face. Upon completion, the sculpture reached 20 meters high and 57 meters long; it's wearing a crown, with the word "cobra" engraved on its forehead, and comes with long, drooping beard on its lower jaw— a sign of the monarch. If you are unable to imagine how big the sculpture is, I can provide you with a specific data—his ears are more than two meters long.

平遥古城
Pingyao Ancient City

近年来风靡剧坛的话剧《立秋》讲述的是丰德票号兴衰的故事：民国初年时局动荡，富甲天下数百年的晋商面临生死存亡的考验，丰德票号在劫难逃，出现了客户挤兑、天津分号被烧、大批国内外借款不能收回的困境，总经理马洪翰恪守祖训为丰德护碑守门，副总经理

话剧《立秋》剧照，山西省话剧院演出
A stage photo from the drama Beginning of Autumn, performed by Shanxi Theatre

许凌翔则主张将丰德票号融入现代银行业的轨道，票号何去何从牵动着观众的心。总经理马洪翰的原型是平遥日升昌票号老板毛鸿翙，副总经理许凌翔的原型是其北京分号经理李宏龄。

The drama *Beginning of Autumn*, sweeping over the stage in recent years is a story about the rise and fall of the Fengde Exchange Shop. In the early years of the Republic of China, the political situation became turbulent, posing great challenges for the survival of Jin (Shanxi) merchants who have remained the wealthiest businessmen in China for hundreds of years. The Fengde Exchange Shop is doomed and caught in a plight: a bank run occurs among its clients; its Tianjin branch is burnt down; moreover, a considerable amount of domestic and foreign loans fail to be recovered. Abiding by the teachings of its forefathers, the general manager Ma Honghan determines to guard Fengde Exchange Shop to its end, while the deputy general manager advocates merging Fengde Exchange Shop into the modern banking system, thus the fate of the Exchange Shop becomes a constant concern of the audience. The prototype of the general manager Ma Honghan is Mao Honghui, the boss of Rishengchang Exchange Shop in Pingyao, and the prototype of the deputy general manager is Li Hongling, the manager of its Beijing branch.

平遥古城是中国保存最完整的一座古代县城，位于山西省中部，始建于西周宣王时期（前827—前782），明洪武三年（1370）扩建，迄今仍完好地保留着明清（1368—1911）时期县城的基本风貌。1997年12月3日，联合国教科文组织在意大利那不勒斯召开的世界遗产委员会第21届大会决定将平遥古城以古代城墙、官衙、街市、民居、寺庙作为整体列入《世界遗产名录》。

平遥古城，李佳琳摄
Pingyao Ancient City, photographed by Li Jialin

平遥古城是依据中国汉民族的文化思想和建筑风格建立起来的，是中原地区古县城的典型代表，至今仍保持着14—18世纪的历史风貌。鸟瞰平遥古城令人感到颇为神奇：整座城池呈龟状，六个城门南北各一，东西各二。城池南门为龟头，门外两眼水井像龟目；北城门为龟尾，是全城的最低处，城内积水都经此流出。平遥东西四座瓮城两两相对，上西门、

Located in the central region of Shanxi Province, the Pingyao Ancient City is the best preserved ancient county seat in China. Originally built in the reign of King Xuan of the Western Zhou Dynasty (827-782 BC), and extended in the third year of Ming Emperor Hongwu (1370), the city still perfectly retains the basic style and features that of counties during the Ming and Qing dynasties. In the 21st session of World Heritage Committee held in Naples, Italy on December 3rd, 1997, UNESCO decided to inscribe the ancient walls, government office, streets, residences and temples of the Pingyao Ancient City as a whole on the World Heritage List.

Constructed according to the cultural elements and architectural styles of the Chinese Han nationality, Pingyao Ancient City is a typical representative ancient county town in the Central Plain region and still retains the historical appearance of that between the 14th to 18th centuries. Looking from a bird's eye view, the city arouses a magical feeling in its viewers: the pattern of the city is shaped as a turtle. There are six city gates, the north and south sides have one gate each, the east and west sides have two gates each. The south gate of the city is the head of the turtle, the two wells outside the gate look like its eyes; the north gate is the tail of the turtle, it's the city's lowest point through which stagnant water inside the city is discharged. Of the four enclosures for defense attached to the east and west city gates, each stands opposite to the other of the same side. The gate of the upper west, lower west and upper east gate

下西门、上东门瓮城城门均向南开，形似龟爪前伸，唯下东门瓮城城门向东开，据说是造城时恐龟爬走，将其左腿拉直拴在距城二十里的麓台上。龟乃长生之物，在古人心目中如同神灵，古人希冀借神龟之力使平遥坚如磐石，永世长存。

平遥古城的交通脉络由纵横交错的四大街、八小街、七十二条蚰蜒巷构成。四大街分别以东西南北四个方向命名，西大街上有创建于道光四年(1824)的中国第一家票号——日升昌，当时在 30 多个省份设立了分支机构，后来还将业务扩展到日本、新加坡、俄罗斯等国。这里一度成为中国金融业的中心，被誉为"大清金融第一街"。八小街与七十二条蚰蜒巷名称各有由来，有的得名于附近的建筑，如衙门街、书院街、文庙街等，有的得名于当地的大户，如郭家巷、

enclosure invariably face the west, resembling a turtle stretching its claws forward. Only the lower east gate enclosure opens its gate to the east, which is said to be a precaution against the turtle's possible escape by fastening its left leg to a bastion twenty miles away from the city upon construction. As a kind of long-living creature, the turtle occupies a position as important as gods in the eyes of ancient people who hoped to fortify Pingyao as a rock-firm eternal city.

The traffic grid of Pingyao Ancient City consists of four avenues, eight streets and seventy-two lanes. The four avenues are named respectively according to their locations as East, West, South and North Avenue. On the West Avenue stands the first exchange shop of China established in the fourth year of Emperor Daoguang (1824) of the Qing Dynasty—Rishengchang which set up branches in over 30 provinces at that time, and later expanded its business to Japan, Singapore, and Russia, etc. The locale became the center of China's financial industry and was known as the First Financial Street of the Great Qing Dynasty. The names of the eight streets and seventy-two lanes have their own origins, some are named after the buildings nearby such as the Government Office Street, College Street, Confucius Temple Street, etc;

平遥古城街道　*Streets in Pingyao Ancient City*

平遥古城夜景
Night view of Pingyao Ancient City

范家街、马家巷等。

平遥古城民居以四合院为主，大家族会修建二进、三进甚至更大的院落，院落之间多用装饰华丽的垂花门分隔。民间有句俗语说平遥"房子半边盖"，指单坡内落水式房屋，蕴含"四水归堂"或"肥水不流外人田"之意。山西气候干旱，风沙较大，将房屋建成单坡能增加外墙的高度，且临街不开窗户能够有效抵御风沙并保证院落安全，而院内紧凑的布局则显示出对外排斥、对内凝聚的民族性格。

2001 年 9 月 20 日，平遥首届国际摄影节开幕，国内与国际接轨、传统与现代互动，使平遥古城独特的风貌、古朴的民风与形式多样的摄影活动交相辉映，在海内外产生了出乎预

some derive their names from local influential families, for example, Guojia Lane, Fanjia Street, and Majia Lane, etc.

The main type of local residence in Pingyao Ancient City is quadrangle. Those wealthy and influential families built mansions with two or three or even more courtyards. The courtyards are usually separated by lavishly decorated pendant gate with flower patterns. As the folk saying goes, "the houses of Pingyao are built with one side only," which means the houses have only one sloping roof for water to drip inside the courtyard and embody the philosophy of "water from the four sides converging into the courtyard" and "never let rich water flow into others' fields." Shanxi has a dry climate and is susceptible to tremendous sandstorms, by building houses with only one sloping roof the height of the outer wall increases; moreover, the act of not opening windows on the street side helps to effectively withstand the sandstorm and ensure the security of the courtyard; whereas the compact layout within the courtyard manifests the ethnic traits of excluding outsiders and uniting insiders.

On September 20th, 2001, the first Pingyao International Photography Festival was launched, enabling communication between home and abroad, as well as the interaction between tradition and modernity. The unique appearance of Pingyao, the antique, plain folk custom and various forms of photography

料的轰动效应，使平遥这座古城焕发勃勃生机。

events added radiance and beauty to each other, causing an unexpected sensation both in and outside the country, making the ancient city of Pingyao radiate with vitality.

三言两语 A FEW REMARKS

开放了，我们老祖宗留下的东西更有价值了。外国人来平遥看古城墙，走古街道，住古民居，逛古寺庙，参观咱中国银行的老祖宗"票号"，这些遗产都成了实实在在的物质财富和精神财富。

[中国] 雷彩玲，女，民俗宾馆老板

来到平遥古城，给我深刻的第一印象的是那一片高大宽厚的深灰色城墙，带着岁月的厚重感，令人仰望，给人震撼。走在城内，眼前尽是古朴的建筑和店铺，有穿梭时光的感觉。比起人声鼎沸的大街，我更喜欢幽深静谧的小巷。看着如织的游人我不禁想到，这样一座美丽的古城，若是没有这些喧嚣，只是住着一些平凡的人们过着平凡的生活，该有多好。

[中国] 武雷顿，男，研究生

With the opening up of China, things left behind by our ancestors have become even more valuable. Foreigners come to Pingyao to see the ancient city walls, walk on its ancient streets, to stay in ancient residences, visit ancient temples and see the prototype of modern Chinese bank—exchange shop. All these relics have come to be regarded as genuine material and spiritual wealth.

[China] Lei Cailing, female, folk hotel owner

My first deep impression upon arrival in Pingyao Ancient City was the circuit of grand and thick walls laden with history which inspired awe and also shocked my heart. Walking inside the city, my eyes were filled with quaint, simple buildings and shops which made me feel like a time traveler. Compared with streets overflowing with noise, I prefer deep and serene alleys. Looking at the swarming visitors I could not help thinking that, if only there had not been so much noise and only ordinary people who lived a simple life.

[China] Wu Leidun, male, graduate student

小链接 ADDITIONAL INFORMATION

欧洲有许多驰名世界的古城，荷兰的代尔夫特（Delft）就是其中之一。代尔夫特拥有一个至今保留着古代风貌的内城，遍布水道和小桥，和阿姆斯特丹的市中心颇有相似之处，因此也有人称代尔夫特是阿姆斯特丹的缩影。在荷兰的黄金世纪（主要是17世纪），代尔夫特是荷兰东印度公司在荷兰的六个据点之一，也就是在那时中国的瓷器被引入荷兰，并发展成了荷兰著名的代尔夫特青花瓷器。

代尔夫特，刘谦功摄
Delft, photographed by Liu Qiangong

There are many world-renowned ancient cities in Europe, and Delft in Netherlands is one of them. In Delft, there is an inner city which still retains its ancient styles and features. With waterways and bridges spreading everywhere, it greatly resembles downtown Amsterdam, resulting in people's reference to Delft as a microcosm of Amsterdam. In the Golden Centuries of Netherlands (mostly the 17th century), Delft was one of the six bases of the Dutch East India Company. It was at this time that Chinese porcelain was introduced into Netherlands and later developed into the famous blue and white porcelain of Delft.

布达拉宫
The Potala Palace

导入 INTRODUCTION

　　布达拉宫最初是为吐蕃王松赞干布迎娶文成公主建造的。松赞干布是藏族历史上的英雄，他统一藏区，建立了吐蕃王朝。唐贞观十四年（640），他遣大相禄东赞至长安，献金五千两，珍玩数百，向唐朝请婚。太宗许嫁宗女文成公主。文成公主（625-680）至吐蕃后被尊称甲木萨汉公主，聪慧美丽，知书达理，对吐蕃贡献良多。

文成公主
Princess Wencheng

The Potala Palace was originally built for the marriage of Songtsen Gampo, the chief of the Tubo Kingdom and Princess Wencheng of the Chinese Tang Dynasty. Songtsen Gampo is a hero in the history of Tibet, who united Tibet and established the Tubo Kingdom. In the 14th year of Emperor Zhenguan (640), Songtsen Gampo sent his prime minister Ludongtsen as envoy to Chang'an; he offered 250 kilograms of gold and hundreds of curios as tribute to the Tang Dynasty with the petition of a marriage. Emperor Taizong promised to marry his sister Princess Wencheng to Songtsen Gampo. Princess Wencheng (625-680) was honored with the title of Mung-chang Kung-co upon her arrival in Tubo, who was intelligent, beautiful, well-educated and sensible, making considerable contribution to the Tubo Kingdom.

　　布达拉宫的"布达拉"是梵语音译，意思是舟岛，又译作"普陀罗"或"普陀"，原指观世音菩萨所居之岛。布达拉宫在拉萨西北的红山上，整个宫殿依山势而建，海拔3700多

Potala, a transliteration from Sanskrit, meaning island, also transliterated as Putuoluo or Putuo, originally referred to the island where Bodhisattva of Compassion resides. Located on the Red Mountain in the

米，占地面积 36 万余平方米，建筑面积 13 万余平方米，主楼高 117 米，共 13 层，其中宫殿、灵塔殿、佛殿、经堂、僧舍、庭院等一应俱全。

布达拉宫辉煌的宫殿最初兴建于公元 7 世纪，当时吐蕃王松赞干布为迎娶唐朝的文成公主专门在红山之上修建了九层楼宫殿一千间。后来吐蕃王朝灭亡之后，古老的宫堡也大部分毁于战火，直至公元 17 世纪，五世达赖建立噶丹颇章王朝并被清朝政府正式封为西藏地方政教首领后，才开始重建布达拉宫，时间为公元 1645 年。此后历代达赖又相继对其进行修缮和扩建，布达拉宫便有了今日之规模。

布达拉宫是历世达赖喇嘛的居住场所，也是过去西藏地方统治者政教合一的统治中心。从五世达赖起，西藏地区重大的宗教、政治仪式都在此举行，同时也是供奉历世达赖喇嘛灵塔的地方。

northwest of Lhasa, the complex was built reclining against the hill at an altitude of 3,700 m. It covers an area of over 360,000 m^2 and occupies over 130,000 m^2 of building space. The main building stands 117 m high and it has 13 stories comprising palaces, stupas, Buddhist halls, sutra halls, accommodations for monks and courtyards, etc.

The construction of the splendid palaces started in the 7th century. To greet his bride Princess Wencheng of the Tang Dynasty, the then Tubo King Songtsen Gampo had a 9-story palace consisting of 1,000 rooms built on the Red Mountain. Following the collapse of the Tubo Dynasty, most of the ancient palaces were destroyed in the warfare. Reconstruction of the Potala Palace did not start until 1645 when the 5th Dalai Lama founded the Ganden Phodrang Dynasty in the 17th century and was officially conferred as the political and religious leader of Tibet by the Qing Dynasty. Thereafter, repeated

西藏拉萨布达拉宫，耿嘉摄　*The Potala Palace in Tibet, photographed by Geng Jia*

布达拉宫给人最为直接的感受是宫宇叠嶂，错落无穷，与山峦浑然一体。其外观有13层，自山脚蜿蜒而上，直至山顶。整体建筑主要由东部的白宫（达赖喇嘛居住）、中部的红宫（佛殿及历代达赖喇嘛灵塔殿）、西部的白色僧房（为达赖喇嘛服务的亲信喇嘛居住）组成。红宫前有一片白色的墙面为晒佛台，每当佛教节庆之日，大幅佛像就悬挂在这里。

白宫是达赖喇嘛的冬宫，也是原西藏地方政府办事机构所在地。位于第四层中央的东有寂圆满大殿是白宫

布达拉宫的墙体（为减轻重量，墙外层是草墙结构），耿嘉摄

The wall of the Potala Palace (the outer layer is made of grass stalks to reduce weight), photographed by Geng Jia

renovation and expansion of the succeeding Dalai Lamas finally brought the palace to its present scale.

As the residence of successive generations of Dalai Lamas, the Potala Palace was also the center of joint political and religious leadership of former Tibetan rulers. Proceeding from the 5th Dalai Lama, the palace has been the location where all major religious rituals and political ceremonies are held, as well as the place where stupas of past Dalai Lamas have been consecrated.

The overwhelming experience the Potala Palace gives to its visitors is the overlapping and endlessly scattered palaces that form an integrated mass with the mountain range. Looking from outside, the palace has 13 stories winding uphill from the foot to the top of the mountain. The whole complex consists of the White Palace in the south (living quarters of Dalai Lama), the Red Palace in the middle (Buddhist halls and stupas of generations of Dalai Lamas) and accommodations for monks in the west (residence of trusted lamas serving the Dalai Lama). In front of the Red Palace is erected a white wall on which large Buddha images are hung during Buddhist festivals.

The White Palace is the winter palace of the Dalai Lama as well as the former office building of the Tibetan local government. The Great Eest Hall located in the middle of the fourth floor is the biggest hall in the White Palace. It is the place where Dalai Lama sits on his throne and performs grand

布达拉宫内景   *Interiors of the Potala Palace*

最大的殿堂，达赖喇嘛在此坐床，并举行亲政大典等重大宗教仪式和政治活动。

红宫主要是达赖喇嘛的灵塔殿和各类佛殿。其中的西有寂圆满大殿是五世达赖喇嘛灵塔殿的享堂，也是布达拉宫最大的殿堂，内壁绘有五世达赖喇嘛赴京觐见清顺治皇帝的壁画。殿内达赖喇嘛宝座上方悬挂着乾隆皇帝御书的"涌莲初地"匾额。法王洞是吐蕃时期遗存的布达拉宫最早的建筑，内有松赞干布、文成公主等人的塑像。

作为藏传佛教的圣地，每年到布达拉宫的朝圣者及观光客不计其数。他们一般由山脚无字石碑起，经曲折石铺斜坡路，直至绘有四大金刚巨幅

religious and political ceremonies such as enthronement, etc.

The Red Palace mainly consists of stupa halls for the Dalai Lama and all kinds of Buddhist halls. As the biggest hall in the Potala Palace, the Great West Hall is the ancestral hall of the 5th Dalai Lama's stupa hall. Murals depicting the 5th Dalai Lama's visit to Emperor Shunzhi of the Qing Dynasty in Beijing were painted on the inner walls of the hall. Above Dalai Lama's throne in the hall, there hangs a plaque bearing the writings of Emperor Qianlong "涌莲初地" which means "the headstream of Buddhism". The Dharma Cave is the earliest building surviving from the Tubo Dynasty. In the cave are sculptures of Songtsen Gampo and Pricess Wencheng and other people.

As the sacred place of Tibetan Buddhism, the Potala Palace attracts numerous pilgrims and visitors each year. They usually set out from

壁画的东大门，并由此通过厚达 4 米的宫墙隧道进入大殿，观喇嘛教真境，悟喇嘛教真谛。

the monument without any word at the foot of the mountain, walking along the sloping path paved with stones until reaching the East Gate painted with gigantic murals of the Four Heavenly Kings; from here, they pass through the 4-meter thick palace wall and finally enter the Great Hall where they mediate upon the truths and ultimate value of Lamaism.

三言两语 A FEW REMARKS

提起西藏，很多人都会想到两个字：神秘。没错儿，我就是怀着这样一种心情奔赴布达拉宫的。一路颠簸之后，我看到了那神秘庄严的古老宫殿，听到了悠扬动听的藏族音乐，尤其是身披红色袈裟的喇嘛用粗犷浑厚的嗓音吟诵佛经很具有震撼力，只有身临其境才能感受到那种奇特的感觉。

[中国] 汪洋，男，工人

Many people would think of the word "mysterious" when mentioning Tibet, indeed, I went to the Potala Palace with such kind of feeling. After a bumpy ride, I finally saw the mysterious and solemn ancient palace, and heard the melodious Tibetan music. Particularly, the rough, deep and resonant voice produced by Lamas in red cassock while chanting sutras has a very shocking effect. It's a strange feeling which can only be experienced by going there in person.

[China] Wang Yang, male, worker

出租车刚刚驶进拉萨市区，布达拉宫的侧影就出现了，远远看去很雄伟、很漂亮。以前我只在杂志中看到过布达拉宫，如今她就活脱脱出现在我眼前，真是一个巨大的惊喜！在这里我就像个小学生，对我来说，一切都很新鲜。

[马来西亚] 艾达，女，公司职员

The silhouette of the Potala Palace appeared in my eyes as soon as the taxi drove into Lhasa City. Looking from a distance, it appears so magnificent and beautiful. I only saw the Potala Palace in the magazines before, but it's right in front of my eyes now, what a big surprise! Here, I'm just like a school pupil, everything is so new to me.

[Malaysia] Ada, female, company employee

小链接 ADDITIONAL INFORMATION

　　在著名导演冯小刚 2004 年拍摄的贺岁片《天下无贼》中，有一组女主角王丽（刘若英饰）朝拜布达拉宫的镜头：背景是绵延起伏的山峦，周围是衣着华丽的藏胞，面对雄伟壮观的布达拉宫，王丽双手合十，一脸虔诚的表情，仿佛进入了无我的境界……布达拉宫就是这样一个圣洁的地方，它能荡涤人们的灵魂，升华人们的感情。

电影《天下无贼》剧照
A still from the movie A World Without Thieves

In the 2004 new year movie *A World Without Thieves* directed by the famous director Feng Xiaogang, there are a few scenes of the heroine Wang Li worshipping the Potala Palace. With the rolling hills as background and also surrounded by gorgeously dressed Tibetans, facing the majestic Potala Palace, Wang Li puts on a pious expression with hands folded, looking as if forgetting her own existence. The Potala Palace is such a holy and pure place that it purifies our spirit and sublimates our emotions.

Living in China

生活在中国

餐桌礼仪
Dinner Etiquette

　　"八仙桌"是一种用来吃饭饮酒的大方桌，可以围坐八个人，是中国家庭中最实用的家具。"八仙桌"名字的由来与道教有关。在道教传说中有八位凡人得道的神仙，分别代表着男、女、老、少、富、贵、贫、贱，人们称他们为"八仙"。他们本领超强，个性与百姓较为接近，是道教中相当重要的神仙代表。

八仙桌
Baxian table

The *baxian* table is a kind of square table used when eating and drinking wine. The table allows eight people to sit around it, which is the most practical furniture in Chinese families. The origin of the name of *baxian* table is related to Taoism. In the Taoist legend, there are eight human beings who attained *Tao* thus becoming immortals representing respectively male, female, old, young, wealth, honor, poverty, and cheap, and were referred to as the Eight Immortals ("八仙" in Chinese) Though endowed with immense magical power, they still share the temperament of common people, and thus regarded as extremely prominent representatives of Taoism immortals.

　　自古以来，中国人不仅把饮食看作是非常重要的事，而且把它与礼仪结合在一起。与西餐多用长桌不同，中餐多用圆桌或方桌，用餐时菜放在桌子中间，大家一起分享。这种习俗在中国已沿袭了几千年，因为它符合

From time immemorial, Chinese people have not only regard food and drinks as very important things, but also associate them with various rituals. Different from rectangular tables used in western meals, tables in Chinese meals are usually round or square ones with dishes placed in the middle, enabling

中国人重视家族和群体关系的传统，在体现家庭伦理、沟通人际关系方面起着重要作用。

圆桌，刘谦功摄
A round table, photographed by Liu Qiangong

中餐坐席在安排上有上首、下首之分。上首即主位，一般来说，面对门的位子是主位，要让给长者或主宾。如果客人较多，那么长辈或地位高的人坐在主位，其余的人按照顺序从左到右交错排列，左边为二、四、六，右边为三、五、七，等等。

中国人有"先酒后饭"的礼俗，即先喝酒，后吃饭。为了让客人喝得尽兴，主人会反复敬酒、劝酒。做法是：先将对方的酒杯斟满，再把自己的酒杯倒满，然后与客人碰杯、干杯。如果客人一饮而尽，主人会非常高兴，宴席的气氛也会更加活跃。在与长辈或地位高的人碰杯时，敬酒的人一般

everybody to share the food. This custom has been carried on for thousands of years, for it is compatible to the Chinese tradition that emphasizes family and group relationships, and plays a prominent role in displaying family ethics and enhancing interpersonal relationships.

The seats in a Chinese meal are classified into *shangshou* (primary seat) and *xiashou* (secondary seat). *Shangshou* is the most important position which generally refers to the seat facing the door; this seat should be offered to seniors or the primary guest. If there are many guests present, the seniors or high-ranked people would sit in the primary position, others would sit alternately on the left and right side of the primary position according to the sequence; the left side includes the 2nd, 4th and 6th positions, while the right side includes the 3rd, 5th and 7th positions.

According to the etiquette, Chinese people would drink wine prior to eating. In order to let the guests drink to their hearts' content, the host would repeatedly propose a toast and urge the guests to drink. Before filling up his own glass, the toastmaster would first charge the glass of the guest, and then clink the glasses while drinking a toast to the guest. If the guest empties his or her cup in one gulp, the host would feel honored, adding to the liveliness of the banquet atmosphere.

敬酒
Toasting

When clinking glasses with se-niors or people with high social positions, the toastmaster would conventionally hold the rim of his glass lower than that of the toastee's, which is a sign of respect and humbleness.

Chopsticks and spoons are widely used in Chinese meals. People utilize chopsticks or spoons with their right hand, while carrying the bowl or plate using their left hand. There are many eating etiquettes at Chinese tables, for instance, the guests will not pick the dishes until being invited by the host; people would not pick dishes from a distant plate; never keep on picking one's favorite dish; don't stand in other people's way while picking; never stick the chopsticks vertically in the bowl which is only a practice while offering sacrifices to gods or ancestors. As all of the people at the table share dishes with each other, people would use serving chopsticks and spoons to take food onto their bowls and plates before eating.

During a Chinese feast, the host would enthusiastically offer food for the guests, hoping them to eat more. The guests should accept with politeness and show their thanks. Even if the host offers something that the guests don't like to eat, the guests should not reject it but they can put them aside instead. At the end of the meal, people would raise their glasses and say some words with good wishes.

会让自己的杯口低于对方的杯口，以表示尊敬和谦虚。

吃中餐主要用筷子和勺子，使用方法是用右手持筷或勺，左手端碗或托碟子。中国人吃饭有许多礼俗，比如：主人邀请客人用餐后客人才可以动筷夹菜；不从远离自己的盘子中夹菜；不用筷子在盘子里挑拣自己喜欢吃的菜；夹菜时不能妨碍别人；不要把筷子插在碗中——这种方式只有祭祀时才使用。由于一桌人共用一桌菜，因此夹菜或盛汤时应使用公筷或公勺放入自己的碗碟中再吃。

在中餐宴席上，主人往往会热情地为客人夹菜，不停地劝客人多吃。对此客人要友好地接受并表示感谢，即使对方给自己夹了不喜欢吃的菜也不要拒绝，可以放在一边。一般散席时大家会共同举杯，说一些表示美好祝愿的话。

三言两语 A FEW REMARKS

中国人很看重餐桌礼仪，我记得小时候吃饭的规矩很多，例如：夹菜不能从别人的手上过啊；不能盯着同一个菜吃，哪怕再喜欢也不行；不能挑挑拣拣，夹到哪块就吃哪块；咀嚼、喝汤都不能发出声音；等等，好多呢。还有长辈没动筷子之前，我们是不准先吃的。吃饱了，一定要打声招呼才能离开餐桌。这些行为随着年龄的增长都成为一种习惯了，不用刻意去遵守，自然而然就会那么做了。

[中国] 陈丽娜，女，公司职员

我对中国的餐桌礼仪很感兴趣。在中国，主人请客人吃饭时至少要做十几个菜，而且要双数，说是图个吉利。这么多菜放在方桌上吃起来不方便，于是就出现了有转盘的圆桌，围坐在周围的客人可以转动转盘让想吃的菜出现在自己面前，这样吃起来就很方便了。主人会让客人首先入座，请长者或客人先动筷子。有的主人还用公筷为客人夹菜，以表示热情好客。席间可以和邻座小声聊几句风趣的话，以调节气氛和增进友谊。吃完饭离席时，不能忘了向主人道声感谢，这是应有的礼节。

[韩国] 陈圣熙，女，研究生

Chinese place much emphasis on dinner etiquette. I can still remember the many rules of eating in my childhood, for example: don't let your dish pass over others' hands while picking; don't keep on eating the same dish, no matter how you love it; don't pick too much, take whatever you grab; don't make sound while chewing food or drinking soup, etc. There are so many of them. We are not allowed to eat unless our seniors start eating. When you get full, you have to greet people present at the table before leaving. These acts become a kind of habit with the growth of my age, there is no need to remind oneself to obey them, for we can naturally observe these rules.

[China] Chen Lina, female, company employee

I am very interested in Chinese dinner etiquette. In China, while inviting guests to dinner, the host would prepare a dozen dishes; they often come in even numbers, which is regarded as auspicious. It's inconvenient to eat as there are so many dishes on the table, so the revolving table was invented. People sitting around the table can revolve the huge disk to get the dish they want to eat, which becomes very convenient while eating. The host would first offer seats to the guests and invite the seniors or guests to start eating. Some hosts serve dishes to their guests using the serving chopsticks to show their hospitality. During the meal, people can have some humorous small talk with the persons nearby to enhance their friendship. Before leaving the table after a meal, remember to say thanks to the guest(s), for it is an expected etiquette.

[South Korea] Jin Seony Hee, female, graduate student

小链接 ADDITIONAL INFORMATION

西餐餐具以刀叉为主，摆放方式为左叉右刀。主刀、鱼刀、汤勺等放在盘子右侧，刀口朝向盘子；主叉、鱼叉等放在盘子左侧，叉头向上。与中餐不同，西餐席位以右为上，主人席位通常安排在席台上方正中，主宾席安排在主人席位的右边，副主宾席安排在主人席位的左边，其他客人则从右至左依次排列。

西餐餐具
Tableware in Western meals

Knives and forks are the main tableware in a Western meal, the fork is placed to the left of the dinner plate while the knife to the right. The main knife, fish knife and spoon are placed to the right of the plate, the blades of the knives are turned toward the plate; the main fork and fish fork are placed to the left of the plate, pointed upward. As different from a Chinese meal, the right side is taken as the primary position in a Western meal. The host's seat is usually arranged in the middle, the seat for the primary guest is placed on the right of the host's, the seat for the secondarily important guest is on the left of the host's, while the rest of the guests sit from right to left in sequence.

茶文化
Tea Culture

导入 INTRODUCTION

茶是中国的"国饮"。汉字中有一个谜语，谜面是"人在草木中"，谜底就是"茶"。唐代（618—907）以前，茶有"荼"、"槚"、"荈"等不同名称，唐代以后简化为"茶"字。

Tea is the "national beverage" of China. There is a riddle in the Chinese language saying "a person inside the grass and plant", and the answer is "tea". Before the Tang Dynasty (618-907), tea had a number of different names such as "tu", "jia", "chuan", etc. They were all simplified into "cha" after the Tang Dynasty.

"人在草木中"
"A person inside the grass and plant"

中国是茶的故乡，种茶、饮茶都有悠久的历史。中国人认为茶是炎帝神农发现的。神农是中国远古时代的一位帝王，传说他不但教民播种五谷，而且发明了陶器和炊具。为了考察对人类有用的植物，神农曾遍尝百草以致中毒，后来发现了茶才得以解毒。

汉代（前206—公元220）以前，茶主要是作为药物使用的。茶作为饮品的正式记载见于汉代典籍，当时有许多地方开始种茶，并且把

As the homeland of tea, China has a long history of tea-growing and drinking. Chinese people attribute the discovery of tea to Yan Emperor Shennong, a legendary ruler of ancient China who not only taught people cultivation of the five grains but also invented pottery and kitchenware. In his exploration of plants beneficial to human beings, Shennong was poisoned after tasting all the plants. It was not until he found out the detoxification power of tea that he was finally saved.

Before the Han Dynasty (206 BC-AD 220), tea mainly served a medical function. Records of tea as a formal beverage appeared

茶叶作为商品买卖。魏晋南北朝时期（220—581）饮茶风俗盛行，茶在士大夫阶层以及文人雅客的生活中成为待客佳品。到了唐代，饮茶不仅深入到社会各个阶层，而且被人们当作一种艺术活动，这一时期产生了世界上第一部关于茶的专著——陆羽的《茶经》。这本书系统总结了唐代及以前的制茶工艺以及煎茶、饮茶的方法，从而加深了人们对茶的认识，推动了品茶艺术的发展。

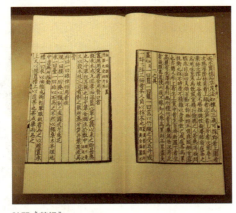

陆羽《茶经》
The Book of Tea by Lu Yu

在中国，茶不仅是一种饮料，而且是一种文化。中国很多地方都出产茶叶，茶的种类也很多，如绿茶、红茶、黄茶、白茶、黑茶、花茶、乌龙茶等。一般说来，江浙人爱喝绿茶，东北人爱喝花茶，福建人爱喝乌龙茶。中国有56个民族，受气候、环境和生产生活方式的影响，一些民族形成了独特的饮茶习俗，如蒙古族的奶茶、藏族的酥油茶等。

中国有"宁可三日无粮，不可一日无茶"的俗话，许多地方都有

in books of the Han Dynasty when tea was grown in many places and traded as a kind of commodity. During the Northern and Southern dynasties (220-581), the custom of tea drinking prevailed; tea became an ideal product of entertaining guests among the literati and officialdom. With the approach of the Tang Dynasty, tea drinking had not only penetrated all levels of society, but also was regarded by people as a kind of artistic activity. It was during this period that the first monograph on tea, *The Book of Tea* by Lu Yu was written. The book systematically summarized the technique of tea-making and methods of tea-baking and tea-drinking both in and before the Tang Dynasty, which deepened people's understanding of tea and pushed forward the development of the art of tea-savoring.

In China, tea is not only a kind of beverage, but also a form of culture. Tea is produced in many parts of China with various kinds, such as green tea, black tea, yellow tea, white tea, dark tea, scented tea and oolong, etc. Generally speaking, people in Jiangsu and Zhejiang provinces like to drink green tea and people from the northeast of China prefer scented tea, while people from Fujian Province like oolong. Among the 56 ethnic

茶　Tea

早晚饮茶的习惯，比如在广东，老年人爱在家喝早茶，年轻人则喜欢去茶楼饮晚茶。饮茶有很多好处：首先可以保健，其次可以娱乐休闲，再者还可以陶冶性情。客来敬茶是中国人的传统，给客人倒茶时不能倒得太满，俗话说："茶满欺人，酒满敬人。"

minorities of China, influenced by distinct climates, environments, ways of production and living, some have developed their own unique tea-drinking customs such as the milk tea of inner Mongolians and the butter tea of Tibetans and so on.

As a popular saying in China goes, "I'd rather do three days without food, but cannot stand a single day without tea." People in many places keep the habit of drinking tea in the morning and at night, for example in Guangdong Province, the old people enjoy drinking tea in the morning at home, while young people prefer drinking evening tea in the teahouse. Drinking tea brings people a lot of benefits: in the first place, it's good for the health; in addition, it's a kind of entertainment; moreover, it can also cultivate people's temperament. Serving tea to the guests is a Chinese tradition. The tea cannot be poured too full, because according to the old saying "a full cup of tea is offensive to the guests while a full glass of wine shows respect to them."

Numerous teahouses, no matter big or small, are scattered all over Chinese cities and the countryside. The Lao She Teahouse in Beijing is named after the modern Chinese writer Lao She and his famous

老舍茶馆内景，刘谦功摄
Interiors of the Lao She Teahouse, photographed by Liu Qiangong

中国城乡各地分布着大大小小的茶馆。在北京有一家老舍茶馆，是以中国现代作家老舍及其著名话剧《茶馆》命名的，1988 年开业以来已接待了 70 余位外国领导人、众多社会名流以及 300 多万中外游客，成为展示中国文化的窗口和促进中外友谊的桥梁。

play *Teahouse*. Ever since its opening in 1988, it has received more than 70 foreign leaders, multiple socialites as well as over 3,000,000 domestic and foreign tourists, making it a window displaying Chinese culture and a bridge enhancing China's friendship with other countries in the world.

三言两语 A FEW REMARKS

作为"柴米油盐酱醋茶"开门七件事之一，茶与中国人的生活息息相关。茶不仅能止渴消食，明目益神，还别有一番意趣。既可以独自一人选择雅静之处，泡上一壶好茶领略"偷得浮生半日闲"之乐，又可以约上三五好友品茶聊天儿。爱茶之人可在缕缕茶香之中畅游神思，回归一颗平静、淡远之心。

[中国] 王盈，女，研究生

在我们国家喝茶不论季节，几乎每个家庭在餐后都要喝茶。如果让我谈对茶的感受，首先我觉得茶是人类文明的标志。据我观察，各国人都有自己偏爱的饮料，如德国人和丹麦人爱喝啤酒，苏格兰人和俄罗斯人爱喝威士忌，意大利人和阿根廷人爱喝葡萄酒，中国人、日本人和韩国人都爱喝米酒和清酒，巴西人爱喝咖啡……但几乎没有一个国家的人不爱茶！茶传播到一个国家就能很快受到当地人民的欢迎，成为生活中不可缺少的饮料，这不正说明了茶是全人类的饮品吗？

[摩尔多瓦] 牙科布·季姆丘克，男，前驻华大使

Tea, as one of the seven basic daily necessities (firewood, rice, oil, salt, soy sauce, vinegar and tea), is closely related to the life of Chinese people. Tea can not only quench one's thirst, help with digestion and improve one's eyesight, but also brings a taste of comfort. You can either secure yourself in a tranquil place, brew a kettle of tea to taste the delight of "snatching some leisure from a busy life"; or you can invite several close friends and chat with each other while savoring tea. The tea, with its fragrance, enables its lovers to soar freely in their mental world, recapturing peace and tranquility of mind.

[China] Wang Ying, female, graduate student

In our country, we drink tea regardless of the season. Almost every family drinks tea after meal. If you ask me about my feeling towards tea, I would say it's the sign of human civilization. According to my own observation, people in different countries have their own favorite drinks. For example, the Germans and Danish favor beer, Scottish and Russians whiskey, Italians and Argentines wine, the Chinese, Japanese and Koreans rice wine and sake, Brazilians coffee. But there is hardly a country whose people don't like drinking tea! As long as introduced into another country, tea will quickly gain popularity among local people, becoming an indispensable drink in daily life. Isn't this the proof of tea as the universal drink of mankind?

[Mildova] Iacob Timciuc, male, former ambassador to China

小链接 ADDITIONAL INFORMATION

　　咖啡与茶、可可并称世界三大饮料。最早的咖啡树源自非洲埃塞俄比亚一个名叫卡法（kaffa）的小镇，后来传到也门和阿拉伯半岛。15世纪以后咖啡逐渐传入埃及、叙利亚、伊朗、土耳其等国，16—17世纪咖啡被作为一种新型饮料引进西方人的生活。18—19世纪中叶咖啡种植在中南美洲得到普及，19世纪末咖啡由法国传教士带入中国云南。20世纪中叶，位于中国海南的兴隆华侨农场大力种植咖啡，使兴隆咖啡名声远扬。2006年兴隆咖啡被评为中国国家地理标志性产品。

Coffee, tea and cocoa are referred to as the top three drinks in the world. The earliest coffee tree originated from a small town called Kaffa in Ethiopia, Africa, and was later introduced into Yemen as well as Arabia. After the 15th century, coffee gradually spread to countries such as Egypt, Syria, Iran, Turkey, etc., and was introduced into western life as a new kind of beverage during the 16th-17th centuries. In the period between the 18th century and the mid-19th century, the growth of coffee was popularized in Central and South America, and was introduced into Yunnan Province, China by a French missionary at the end of the 19th century. In the mid-20th century, the Xinglong Farm of Overseas Chinese located in China's Hainan Province started to grow coffee on a massive scale, which gained the farm worldwide reputation. In 2006, Xinglong Coffee was rated as a product of geographical indication.

北京蓝色港湾的咖啡馆，田琨摄　　*Café in Solana Mall of Beijing, photographed by Tian Kun*

中国服饰
Chinese Style Clothing

导入 INTRODUCTION

　　近年来，随着中国经济的快速发展，中国人的衣食住行越来越多地受到外来文化的影响，另一方面也出现传统回归的现象，"汉服运动"的兴起就是其中之一。"汉服运动"的全称是"汉服复兴运动"，以青少年族群为主体，通过在婚礼、成年礼、毕业典礼等隆重仪式上身穿汉族传统服饰，弘扬民族传统文化。上图为一些年轻人身着汉服参加成人礼。

With the rapid economic development of China in recent years, the basic necessities of life, including food, clothing, shelter and transportation of Chinese people are increasingly influenced by foreign cultures. On the other hand, however, there are also signs of return to tradition and the *hanfu* movement is one of them. The full name of the campaign is the Movement of Reviving Han Chinese Clothing mainly undertaken by teenagers who wear traditional Han Chinese clothing on occasions such as weddings, initiation into adulthood, and graduation ceremonies, etc., all in order to promote and develop national culture. On the left is a picture of teenagers dressed in Han Chinese clothing, who are participating in the adulthood ceremony.

　　中国是丝绸的故乡。传说远古时期，黄帝的妃子嫘祖发明了养蚕织丝的方法，从此中国人开始用丝绸制作衣裳。

China is the homeland of silk. As the legend goes, Leizu, a concubine of the Yellow Emperor, invented methods of rearing silkworms and weaving silk. From then on,

深衣
Long robe

中国传统服饰的基本形制是上衣下裳、上下连属，这种样式在先秦时期（前21世纪—前221）就已确定了。春秋战国时期（前770—前256）最为流行的服饰是深衣，这种上下一体的服装样式对中国古代服饰文化产生了深远影响。中国是一个多民族国家，服饰始终融合了多民族的文化因素，呈现出丰富多彩的面貌，如春秋时期的赵武灵王为富国强兵而推行"胡服骑射"，不仅加强了民族关系，同时也丰富了汉族的服装样式。

Chinese people started to make clothes by using silk as raw material.

The basic form of traditional Chinese clothing, conventionalized in the Pre-Qin Period (21st century BC–221 BC) is represented by the upper garment and lower skirt which are joined together as an integrated item. The most popular clothing during the Spring and Autumn and Warring States Period was a long robe. The clothing design, with its upper and lower parts joined to form a whole, had a profound influence on the ancient Chinese clothing culture. In a multiethnic country such as China, clothing has always been a fusion of multiple ethnic cultures, presenting a rich and colorful appearance. For example, King Wuling of Zhao Kindom in the Spring and Autumn Period implemented the policy of wearing clothes of the northern ethnic minorities and learning to shoot on horseback. The policy not only strengthened ethnic relationships but also enriched the forms of Han Chinese clothing.

The traditional Chinese clothing is typically represented by loose robes with wide sleeves, and possesses a style of dynamic elegance. Upon initiation into the modern times, the *zhongshan* suit and *qipao* which combine Chinese and Western cultural elements gradually established themselves as the typical examples of Chinese clothing. The *zhongshan* suit derived its name from Dr. Sun Yat-sen, leader of the Revolution of 1911[1]; the design is assigned with a political significance as well as symbolic meaning. The four pockets

① The Revolution of 1911 refers to the Chinese bourgeois democratic revolution that broke out in 1911, the third year of Xuantong Reign of the Qing Dynasty, which terminated the Chinese feudal society having lasted for over 2,000 years.

中国传统服饰以宽袍大袖为主，风格飘逸洒脱。近代以后，融合了中西文化因素的中山装和旗袍逐渐成为中国服饰的代表样式。"中山装"的名称由辛亥革命①领导者孙中山先生的名字而来，其设计富于政治色彩和象征意义。中山装前襟的四个口袋分别代表礼、义、廉、耻，五粒纽扣象征行政、立法、司法、考试、监察五权分立，袖口的三个扣子则为三民主义——民族、民权、民生。

旗袍的改制始于20世纪20年代，流行于20世纪30—40年代，在满族妇女服饰的基础上融合了西方服饰元素，最终形成了一种"中西合璧"的新型女装样式。旗袍既体现了东方女性的含蓄典雅，又具有欧洲女装的曲线之美，因而一度成为中国都市女性的最爱。

图案是服饰的构成要素之一，往往具有某种象征意义。中国传统服饰

中山装
Zhongshan suit

in the front of the suit represent respectively propriety, justice, honesty and honor; the five buttons symbolize separation of the five powers: executive, legislative, judicial, examining and monitoring; the three cuff-buttons symbolize the Three Principles of the People: nationalism, democracy and people's livelihood.

Qipao was reformed since the 1920s and became popularized from the 1930s to 1940s. As a result of the incorporation of Western clothing elements into Manchu women's clothing, *qipao* eventually emerged as a new type of female garment that combines Chinese and Western elements. *Qipao* not only embodies the subtlety and elegance of oriental women but

中国旗袍展示，刘谦功摄
Qipao, photographed By Liu Qiangong

---

① 辛亥革命：指 1911 年（清宣统三年）中国爆发的资产阶级民
　主革命，这次革命结束了中国长达两千年之久的封建社会制度。

上常有龙、凤、鹤、麒麟、鸳鸯等各种吉祥动物的图案，也有萱草、牡丹等各种吉祥花卉的图案，还有日、月、大海、云、山等自然景观的图案。这些图案的主题在很大程度上反映了中国远古时代的风俗和信仰，特别是自然崇拜的观念。除上述动物、植物、自然景观等图案外，最能体现中国文化特色的还有文字图案，常见的有"回、万、福、寿、喜、富贵平安、吉祥如意"等字样，这些图案直接用汉字表达了人们的美好愿望。

服装上的龙、凤图案
Dragon and phoenix patterns on clothing

also displays the beauty of feminine curves belonging to European women's clothing, which has secured its status as the favorite garment of urban Chinese women once upon a time.

Patterns are an essential constituting element of clothing and usually hold certain symbolic meaning. Traditional Chinese clothes are often ornamented with patterns of auspicious animals such as dragons, phoenixes, cranes, kylins, mandarin ducks, etc., and auspicious flowers such as the day lilies and peonies, as well as natural landscape objects such as the sun, moon, ocean, clouds, and mountains, etc. The theme of these patterns reflects to a considerable extent the customs and beliefs of ancient China, especially the worship of nature. In addition to the above-mentioned patterns of animals, plants and landscape objects, there are also patterns of Chinese characters which best represent the uniqueness of Chinese culture, such as "回" (coming back), "万" (ten thousand), "福" (blessing), "寿" (longevity), "喜" (happiness), "富贵平安" (wealthy with honor and security), "吉祥如意" (auspicious and lucky), etc. Such patterns express people's good wishes directly in Chinese characters.

三言两语
A FEW REMARKS

　　我在中国工作，以前每年回日本前都要买旗袍作为礼物送给亲朋好友。后来我在北京路光明广场发现了一家名叫"汉尚华莲"的汉服店，面对那些美丽的大气的衣裳，我感到十分震撼，有一种似曾相识的感觉。店主热情地向我介绍了汉服的概念和基本特点。那时我才知道原来汉服是中国传统服饰更早的代表，从那以后我经常买汉服作礼物赠送

As I work in China, I used to buy *qipao* as presents for my relatives and friends every year before going back to Japan. Later, I found a shop selling Han Chinese clothing with the name of Han Shang Hua Lian. I was shocked at the sight of the gorgeous and magnificent clothing, attaining a sense of déjà vu. The shop owner introduced the basic concepts and features of Han Chinese clothing to me in a friendly manner. It was not until then that I realized Han Chinese clothing is a much earlier representation of traditional Chinese clothing. From then on, I have

给我的亲朋好友。

[日本] 石川，女，记者

　　我最喜爱的传统服饰是旗袍，它很能突出女性的曲线美，而且所衬托出的美感含蓄、不张扬，这正是中国女性的独特之美。此外我也很喜欢唐装，因为唐装中包含有很多中华文化元素，节日时穿着让人感到非常喜庆。

[中国] 王芊卉，女，研究生

often purchased Han Chinese clothing as presents for my relatives and friends.

[Japan] Ishikan, female, journalist

My favorite traditional clothing is *qipao*, because it highlights the beautiful curves of women; moreover, the implicit, humble beauty set off by *qipao* is precisely unique to Chinese women. Besides *qipao*, I'm also fond of Tang suits, for they contain many Chinese cultural elements. I feel very happy if I wear them during festivals.

[China] Wang Qianhui, female, graduate student

小链接 ADDITIONAL INFORMATION

　　中国的"丝绸之都"在杭州，法国的"丝绸之都"是里昂。里昂位于法国东南部，是法国第三大城市。丝绸纺织业在里昂城市发展史中曾占有重要地位。16世纪以前，欧洲最大的丝绸产地是意大利。1536年，在法国王室的支持下，里昂设立了第一个丝绸纺织作坊，并专门从意大利聘请来熟练的工匠。丝织业很快成为里昂最重要的手工业，也为这座城市带来了巨大的财富。到17世纪，里昂已成为欧洲最重要的丝绸产地。在里昂有一座丝绸博物馆（musée des tissus），是由昔日的市政府建筑改建的。

Hangzhou is the silk capital of China, and its French counterpart is Lyon. Situated in the southeast of France, Lyon is the third largest city of the country. The silk textile industry once played a prominent role in the development of Lyon. Before the 16th century, Italy was the biggest producer of silk in Europe. In 1536, with support of the French royal family, the first workshop of silk spinning engaging skillful craftsman from Italy was established in Lyon. Silk spinning instantly became the most important handicraft industry of Lyon, creating enormous wealth for the city. In the 17th century, Lyon emerged as the most important silk producer of Europe. In Lyon, there lies a silk museum (musée des tissus) which was reconstructed from the former municipal government office.

Folk Arts

民间工艺

剪 纸
Paper Cutting

相传农历正月初三是"老鼠娶亲"的日子，会听到老鼠吱吱叫的声音。为了不打扰老鼠娶亲，人们会在这个晚上提早熄灯就寝，并在厨房或老鼠经常出入的角落撒上一些食品，与老鼠共享新婚的欢乐和一年的收成，以免得罪老鼠，给来年带来祸患。

剪纸"老鼠娶亲"
The paper cut of The Mice Wedding

Tradition has it that the 3rd day of the first lunar month is the day of the mice wedding when the squeak of mice can be heard. To avoid disturbing their wedding, people would blow out the candles and go to bed earlier than usual. In case of offending the mice, which might bring misfortunes in the following year, people would also scatter food in their kitchens or the corners frequented by mice, hoping to share the joy of marriage and the year's harvest with the mice.

剪纸是中华民族的传统民间工艺，也是世界艺术宝库中的一种珍藏。2010 年，中国剪纸通过联合国教科文组织保护非物质文化遗产政府间委员会审批，被列入《人类非物质文化遗产代表作名录》。

剪纸的产生和流传与中国的节

Paper cutting is a traditional Chinese folk handicraft, which is also valuable in the treasure house of the world's art. In 2010, Chinese paper cutting was approved by UNESCO's Intergovernmental Committee for the Safeguarding of Intangible Cultural Heritage and was added on the Representative List of the Intangible Cultural Heritage of

日风俗有着密切联系，逢年过节人们喜欢把美丽鲜艳的剪纸贴在雪白

巨型剪纸作品《百鸟朝凤》（200cm×200cm），李佳琳摄

The giant paper cut Hundreds of Birds Paying Homage to the Phoenix (200 cm × 200 cm), photographed by Li Jialin

的窗纸或明亮的玻璃窗上，或者墙上、门上、灯笼上，节日的气氛被渲染得异常喜庆与热烈。

据说剪纸从纸一出现便有了。唐代（618—907）剪纸艺术获得了大发展，从现藏于大英博物馆的唐代剪纸可以看出，当时剪纸手工艺术水平极高，画面构图完整，表达了一种天上人间的理想境界。南宋时期（1127—1279）出现了以剪纸为职业的艺人。明清（1368—1911）是剪纸艺术的鼎盛时期，剪纸成为重要的居家装饰品。

由于各地的风俗习惯不同，剪纸的风格也异彩纷呈。构图上，北方简洁古朴，南方繁茂华丽；造型上，

Humanity. The emergence and spread of paper cutting is intricately linked with the customs of Chinese festivals. During Spring Festival or other celebrations, people like to stick beautiful and bright-colored paper cuts on white window paper or crystal glass windows, or on the walls, doors and lanterns to enhance the liveliness and exuberance of the festivals.

It is said that paper cutting has existed ever since the invention of paper. The art of paper cutting witnessed considerable progress during the Tang Dynasty (618-907). This is attested to by the Tang Dynasty paper cuts stored in the British Museum. Facilitated by the superb craftsmanship at that time, the paper cut was shaped as an integral design depicting an ideal status of a world in paradise. Craftsmen choosing paper cutting as their profession appeared in the Southern Song Dynasty (1127-1279). The Ming and Qing dynasties (1368-1911) recorded a period of great prosperity for paper cutting during which paper cuts became important domestic decorations.

The style of paper cuts varies according to different local customs. Motifs of the paper cuts made in the northern China seek out primitive simplicity, while their southern counterparts embrace luxuriance and magnificence; the shaping of those of the north is bold and unconstrained while the southern ones are fine and delicate; lines of the northern paper cuts are bold and forceful while those of the south are fine and smooth; as for style, the northern ones are powerful

北方粗犷豪放，南方细密纤巧；线条上，北方浑厚苍劲，南方细腻流畅；风格上，北方雄壮浑厚，南方秀丽优美。北方剪纸以河北剪纸、山西剪纸、陕西剪纸和山东剪纸为代表；南方剪纸以湖北剪纸、广东剪纸和福建剪纸为代表。

　　河北蔚县被称为"中国剪纸艺术之乡"，是北方剪纸的代表，以窗花见长。中国剪纸绝大部分是用红色或其他单色纸剪成，唯独蔚县剪纸是彩色的。这种剪纸其实不是"剪"，而是"刻"，它以薄薄的宣纸为材料，先用小巧锐利的刻刀刻制，再用毛笔蘸颜料点染上色。蔚县剪纸色彩浓艳、热烈，具有浓郁的乡土气息。

河北蔚县剪纸《喜上梅梢》
A paper cut in Yuxian County of Hebei Province, Magpies on the Tip of the Plum Branch

and vigorous, while the southern ones appear beautiful and graceful. Northern style paper cut is represented by those produced in Hebei, Shanxi and Shandong while the southern style is represented by those produced in Hubei, Guangdong and Fujian.

Yuxian County of Hebei Province, being referred to as the homeland of Chinese paper cutting is representative of northern style paper cuts specializing in window paper cuts. Distinct from most Chinese paper cutting which use red or single-colored paper, the paper cuts of Yuxian comes in multiple colors. In fact, this kind of paper cutting is not cut but engraved by using extremely thin *xuan* paper as material. They are first engraved with a delicate, sharp chisel and then colored with brushes dipping in the paint. Being richly and brightly painted with lively colors, the paper cuts in Yuxian County possess a strong flavor of rural life.

剪纸《五谷丰登》
A paper cut Plentiful Harvest of the Five Grains

民间剪纸的题材多来源于现实生活，剪纸的创作者把他们对生活的热爱和对自然的认识以剪纸这种特殊的艺术形式表现出来，如"双喜字"是中国婚礼必备的符号，"喜鹊登枝"表示喜事降临，"五谷丰登"寓意农业丰收。除了用于窗花、门楣上烘托节日气氛之外，剪纸图样还可以用做刺绣的花样。在现代社会中，剪纸艺术越来越多地用于婚纱设计、时装设计、居家用品设计中，体现出剪纸艺术的实用性和艺术魅力。

Most of the themes of folk paper cuts come from real life. Creators of paper cuts choose to show their enthusiasm towards life and understanding of nature by means of paper cutting. For instance, the "character of double happiness" is an indispensable sign at Chinese weddings; "magpies topping the tree branches" signifies the arrival of happiness; "plentiful harvest of the five grains" symbolizes good harvests of agriculture. Apart from being stuck on windows and lintels to enhance festival atmosphere, designs of paper cutting can also be used as embroidery patterns. In the modern society, paper cutting is increasingly incorporated into the designs of wedding gowns, fashion and household items, displaying its practicality and artistic charm.

三言两语 A FEW REMARKS

剪纸是中国最古老的民间艺术之一，是我们老祖宗智慧的结晶。薄薄的一张纸经过一番修剪，一个个漂亮的图案就出现了，好多外国人都觉得很神奇。可惜的是，现代人的生活节奏越来越快，已经很少有人能够真正坐下来耐心完成一幅费工夫的作品了，不过听说现在小学的手工课有剪纸，大学里面也开什么包括剪纸艺术的才艺课，这可都是好事儿。

[中国] 李桂香，女，民间艺人

Paper cutting is one of the oldest folk arts in China, it's the fruit of our ancestors' wisdom. Seeing a piece of thin paper being cut into beautiful patterns seems so magical to many foreigners. Unfortunately, with the ever-accelerating living pace of modern society, few people would calm down to finish a piece of art work that demands considerable amount of efforts and patience. However, I heard that primary schools offer students handwork lessons teaching paper cutting, and the universities are also providing talent courses on the art of paper cutting. These are all good signs for the future.

[China] Li Guixiang, female, folk artist

我是塞内加尔留学生，来中国以前我没见过剪纸，因为我的国家没有剪纸，所以第一次见到剪纸时我感到很新奇、很有意思，没想到一张纸、一把剪刀可以做出这么好看的艺术品。另外，中国剪纸都是红色的，我知道红色在中国文化中有特别的意义，表示的是喜庆和热烈。

[塞内加尔] 阿布杜，男，大学生

As a foreign student from the Republic of Senegal, I wasn't able to see any paper cuts before I came here. As there is no paper cutting in my country, I felt so surprised at the first sight of an interesting paper cut. I didn't expect they can create such a wonderful work of art using simply a piece of paper and a pair of scissors. Besides, all Chinese paper cuts are red, which I know carries special significance in the Chinese culture implying joy and enthusiasm.

[Republic of Senegal] Abdul, male, college student

剪影 "听琴"
A paper cut, Listening to the Violin

伊丽莎白·巴莱特 (Elizabeth Barrett，1806—1861)，19 世纪英国著名女诗人，其最著名的作品是《葡萄牙人十四行诗集》。全诗 45 幅剪影配图：花前、树下、窗前、梳妆、听琴、读信、郊游、求爱……一幅幅倩影，一个个优美姿态，轮廓清晰，感情丰富，让人感到两颗相爱的心在默默相聚，传递着无形的心声。这些剪影插图为英国的剪影艺术赢得了很高的声誉，同时它们也是完整形象剪影的代表作。

Elizabeth Barrett (1806-1861) is a British female poet of the 19th century whose best work is represented by *Sonnets from the Portuguese*. The collection contains 45 pictures of paper cuts depicting people who are near the flowers, under the trees, beside the window, dressing up, listening to the violin, reading the letters, going on an excursion, courting, etc.; their graceful figures and elegant postures are neatly shaped with embodiment of rich emotions, urging us to feel the silent unification of two loving hearts delivering their intangible inner voices. These paper cuts gained great reputation for British art of paper cutting and still serve as examples of complete and vivid silhouettes of images.

景泰蓝
Chinese Cloisonné

导入 INTRODUCTION

在 1904 年芝加哥世界博览会上，一件非常精美的艺术品——景泰蓝"宝鼎炉"荣膺一等奖，为中国景泰蓝在世界珐琅艺术领域增添了不可磨灭的光彩；继而于 1915 年巴拿马博览会又获金奖，再创辉煌。这是中国的骄傲，也是中国景泰蓝人的骄傲。

In 1904, the Chinese cloisonné Precious Tripod Furnace, an extraordinarily exquisite work of art, was honored the first award at the Chicago World's Fair, rendering the Chinese cloisonné an indelible glory in the field of world enamel art. More exhilaratingly, it was again awarded the golden prize at the 1915 Panama Pacific International Exposition, making Chinese people, especially cloisonné craftsmen proud.

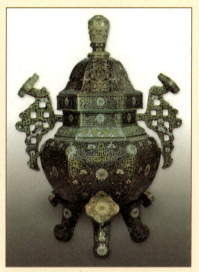

景泰蓝"宝鼎炉"（民国初景泰蓝私立作坊"老天利"所制）

The Chinese cloisonné Precious Tripod Furnace (produced by a private cloisonné workshop named Lao Tian Li in the early years of Republic of China)

景泰蓝又称"铜胎掐丝珐琅"，距今已有 600 多年的历史，是最具北京特色的传统手工艺品之一。景泰蓝的制作是集青铜、陶瓷、绘画、雕塑技艺与国外掐丝珐琅工艺为一体的独特工艺。

景泰蓝作为一种美术工艺品始于明代景泰（1450—1457）年间，

The Chinese cloisonné, or enameled copper base soldered with metal strips, is one of the most distinctive traditional Beijing handicrafts with a history of over 600 years. The production of Chinese cloisonné is a unique craftsmanship that combines Chinese traditional bronze, ceramics, paintings, carving techniques and foreign enamel techniques.

初创时只有蓝色，故名景泰蓝。清乾隆（1736—1796）年间景泰蓝工艺得到了大发展，在风格上不仅继承了早期景泰蓝的古典与雅致，而且开始呈现出纤巧、绮丽的风格特征。

由于景泰蓝制造工艺复杂，釉料配制和烧造技术难度大，生产成本高，因此明清时期（1368—1911）景泰蓝都是皇家专用的器物或饰品，其珍品在很长一段时期也主要是在宫廷中制作的，直到清朝（1616—1911）后期，景泰蓝才作为商品出现在市场上。

清乾隆年间"掐丝珐琅缠枝花卉纹双联瓶"
Chinese cloisonné Double Vases with Interweaving Flowers in Qianlong Period, Qing Dynasty

景泰蓝的生产工艺十分复杂，一个产品要经过十几道工序才能完成，主要有：

第一，设计，主要包括造型设计、纹样设计、彩图设计等。

第二，制胎，即将紫铜片按图裁剪成不同的圆形或扇形，并锤打成各种形状的铜胎。

第三，掐丝与焊丝，即用镊子

The Chinese cloisonné, as a kind of artistic handicraft, dating back to the Jingtai Period (1450-1457) of the Ming Dynasty. With its initial color being blue, the handicraft carries the name Jingtai Blue. During the Qianlong Period (1736-1796), Qing Dynasty, the craftsmanship of Chinese cloisonné was greatly developed; and as for style, it not only inherited the classical and elegant features of early cloisonné, it also began to show delicate and exquisite features.

Due to its complicated manufacturing process, the technical difficulty of preparing enamel paint and firing enamel, and its high production cost, Chinese cloisonné were the articles or decorations used exclusively by the royal families during the Ming and Qing dynasties (1368-1911). Cloisonné of high quality was mainly produced in the imperial court for quite a long time until the late Qing Dynasty (1616-1911) when it began to show up on the market as a commodity.

The manufacturing process of Chinese cloisonné is so complicated that the production of one article needs a dozen working procedures, which include:

First, design, which includes the design of its

掐丝
Inlaying copper wire

将压扁的紫铜丝掐或掰成各种精美的图案花纹，再粘在铜胎上，然后经900℃的高温焙烧将铜丝花纹牢牢焊在铜胎上。

第四，点蓝，即将珐琅釉料依照图案所标示的颜色填入铜丝纹饰框架中。

第五，烧蓝，将填满色釉的胎体放到炉温800℃的炉中烘烧，色釉由砂粒状固体熔化为液体，待冷却

modeling, pattern and color.

Second, base making, i.e. craftsmen firstly cut red copper sheets into round or sector pieces according to the design, and then hammer them into various copper molds.

Third, inlaying and welding copper wire, i.e. craftsmen firstly strip or break the flattened red copper into various exquisite patterns with tweezers, then glue them to the copper molds. After that, they fire them at the high temperature of 900 ℃ so as to firmly solder the copper wire design onto the copper molds.

Fourth, enamel filling, i.e. craftsmen fill enamel paint into the framework of copper wire patterns according to indications in the design.

Fifth, enamel firing, i.e. craftsmen heat the copper base filled with colored enamel in a furnace at 800 ℃. During this step, the sand-like solid colored enamel will melt into liquid, and after cooling, it becomes bright-colored enamel attaching to the base. At this point, as the colored enamel is

磨光　　　*Polishing*

后成为附着在胎体上的绚丽的色釉，此时色釉低于铜丝高度，故需再填色釉，再经烧结。如此反复四五次，直至将纹样内部填到与掐丝纹平齐的程度。

第六，磨光，即用粗砂石、黄石、木炭分三次将凹凸不平的蓝釉磨平，最后用木炭、刮刀将没有蓝釉的铜线、底线、口线刮平磨亮。

第七，镀金。为了防止产品氧化，需将磨平的景泰蓝放入镀金液槽中，然后通上电流，几分钟后黄金液便牢牢附着在景泰蓝的金属部位上了，再经水洗、干燥处理后，一件景泰蓝艺术品才真正完成。

景泰蓝作为中国独特的艺术品在明清时期已开始出口海外，现在也是赠与亲朋好友和国际友人的上好礼品。

lower than the copper wire, craftsmen will refill enamel into the copper base and then heat it again. This procedure will be repeated for four or five times until the colored enamel reached the same height with copper wire patterns.

Sixth, polishing, i.e. craftsmen polish the uneven blue enamel for three times, using coarse emery, yellow stones and charcoal in each step of the process. Finally, by using charcoals and scrapers they scrape smooth and polish the copper wires, base wires and mouth wires to which there is no blue enamel attached.

Seventh, gilding. In order to prevent oxidation of the products, the polished Chinese cloisonné needs to be put into a trough containing gold fluid, then the electric current is applied and after a few minutes, the gold fluid will firmly attach to the metal part of the Chinese cloisonné. Only after washing and drying treatment, a piece of Chinese cloisonné is really completed.

As a unique artwork of China, Chinese cloisonné was exported to overseas in the Ming and Qing dynasties and now has become a first-class present for relatives and friends as well as international friends.

景泰蓝手镯，田琨摄
A Chinese cloisonné bracelet, photographed by Tian Kun

三言两语 A FEW REMARKS

从事景泰蓝制作这个行业的人员越来越少，肯十年磨一剑的年轻人就更少了。这不仅仅是一种工艺品的制造问题，这关系到文化传承与文化审美。现代人的脚步与心都太匆忙，如何回归心灵的精致，让我们的生活更有质量一些，或许可以从静静地欣赏一尊景泰蓝开始。

[中国] 张同禄，男，陶艺家

景泰蓝的每一道工序都需手工完成，精致异常，是很好的藏品，在故宫以及国外的很多大型的博物馆，景泰蓝都有一席之地，供人们观赏，让人们赞叹。然而，现在很多人似乎都对传统工艺不感兴趣，一味追求现代化的奢侈品，实在是很遗憾的事。

[中国] 夏紫薇，女，中学教师

People engaged in Chinese cloisonné production are increasingly few, young people who are willing to spend years of energy and efforts refining his techniques are even fewer. This is not just a problem about the manufacturing of a particular kind of handicraft, but relates to cultural heritage and aesthetics. Since both the pace of life and heart are too hasty for modern people, maybe it is a good start for them to quietly enjoy the delicacy of a piece of Chinese cloisonné to seek inner peace and live a better life.

[China] Zhang Tonglu, male, pottery maker

With all the working procedures of the Chinese cloisonné done manually, the products are every exquisite thus becoming good collections. In the Palace Museum and many other large foreign museums, the Chinese cloisonné always occupies a place for people's admiring. Nowadays, however, many people seem to have little interest in the traditional crafts, and they just blindly pursue modern luxuries, which is really unfortunate.

[China] Xia Ziwei, female, middle school teacher

小链接 ADDITIONAL INFORMATION

清乾隆年间"掐丝珐琅多穆壶"（中国国家博物馆馆藏）

Wire Inlayed Cloisonné Enamel Mdong-Mo Pot in Qianlong Period, Qing Dynasty (reserved in the National Museum of China)

在 2008 年中贸圣佳拍卖公司春季拍卖会上，一对高 28 厘米的清乾隆"掐丝珐琅多穆壶"以 9072 万元人民币成交，创造了中国珐琅器即景泰蓝拍卖价格的世界最高纪录。多穆壶是藏族盛酥油茶的器皿，此件"掐丝珐琅多穆壶"是清乾隆年间宫廷造办处精心制作的宫廷陈设品，造型具有浓郁的民族风格，体现了藏、蒙、满、汉各民族团结一致的精神。

In a spring auction held by Sungari Auction Company in 2008, a pair of 28 cm high Wire Inlayed Cloisonné Enamel Mdong-Mo Pots from the Qianlong Period, Qing Dynasty knocked off 90.72 million yuan, creating a world record auction price amongst Chinese cloisonné. The Mdong-mo pot is a utensil used for butter tea by Tibetans. This pot, as a piece of palace furnishing crafted by the palace workshop, is modeled with strong ethnic style reflecting the unity of Tibetan, Mongolian, Manchu and Han peoples.

Folk Sports
民间运动

空竹
Chinese Yo-Yo

公园里抖空竹
People playing Chinese yo-yo in the park

　　走进中国大大小小的公园，有一种运动几乎随处可见，这就是抖空竹。抖空竹是中国独特的民族体育运动，它不仅是一种锻炼身体的方式，也是一种优美的艺术表演。空竹以竹木为材料制成，中空，因而得名。据文献记载，抖空竹在中国已经有一千七百多年的历史了。

Walking into Chinese parks, no matter big or small, you can see a very popular sport almost everywhere, which is Chinese yo-yo. Chinese yo-yo, a national sport unique to the Chinese people, is not only a way of exercising but also a kind of elegant art performance. Chinese yo-yo is made of bamboo; it gets the name due to its hollow inside. According to the records, the playing of Chinese yo-yo has already witnessed a history of over one thousand and seven hundred years.

　　空竹是用竹木制成的玩具，在圆柱的一端或两端安上周围有几个小孔的圆盒，用绳子抖动圆柱，圆盒便快速旋转并发出声响。

　　空竹分为单轮（木轴一端为圆盘）和双轮（木轴两端各有一圆盘）。圆盘四周的哨口以一个大哨口为低音孔，若干小哨口为高音孔，以各圆盘哨口的数量而分为双响、四响、

Chinese yo-yo is a toy made of bamboo, with several discs having small holes on them fixed to one or both ends of an axle. When you shake the axle with a string, the discs will spin, making a humming sound.

Chinese yo-yo can be divided into single-bell ones and double-bell ones, the former with a disc fixed to only one end of the axle, and the latter with a disc to both ends. The large groove on the disc is responsible for low-

空竹
The Chinese yo-yo

六响，直至三十六响。拽拉抖动时，各哨口同时发出声响，高亢雄浑，声入云霄。

抖空竹时，先将空竹放在右脚尖上，右手将绳子在空竹上绕两圈，然后提起右手杆，再落下，顺势放掉一圈绳子，左手轻提，空竹就起来了。这只是基本功。

抖空竹的花样很多，名字也很有意思，如"金鸡上架"、"翻山越岭"、"织女纺线"、"夜观银河"、"二郎担山"、"抬头望月"、"鲤鱼摆尾"、"童子拜月"、"鹞子翻身"、"海底捞月"、"青云直上"

pitched sound and the rest of the small ones are for high-pitched sound. Chinese yo-yo can also be classified according to the amount of grooves on the rim of the disc, these include 2, 4, 6 and up to 36 grooves. When spun with a string, the grooves concurrently produce a sonorous sound which can be heard at a great distance.

When people play a Chinese yo-yo, they should first place the yo-yo on the tip of their right foot, wind the string twice on the axle, then lift the right stick and then drop it; meanwhile, they should release the string so that it winds around the axle only once, and then gently lift the left hand to make the yo-yo spin. These are only the basics of playing Chinese yo-yo.

Chinese yo-yo can be used to perform many tricks and each enjoys an interesting name, for instance, "golden rooster upon the roost", "over the mountains and ascending the hills", "weaver at work", "watching the milky way at night", "Erlang shouldering the mountain", "raising the head and watching the moon", "the wagging carp", "the child worshipping the moon" and "the somersaulting hawk", "touching reflection of the moon in the water", "soaring

一人抖起七个空竹
A man spinning seven Chinese yo-yos at the same time

等等。最为惊险的是"蚂蚁上树"：
长绳一端系于树梢，另一端手持；
另有一人抖动一只空竹，忽然将飞
转的空竹抛向长绳，持绳者用力拉
动长绳，将空竹抖向高空，可飞上
五六十米的空中。待空竹落下时，
抖空竹者稳稳接住。初见此技者无
不先是大声惊呼，继而热烈鼓掌。

　　抖空竹看上去似乎只是简单的
上肢运动，其实不然，它会将你的
全身都调动起来。抖空竹时注意力
要高度集中，玩儿各种花样时眼睛
要始终跟随着上下翻飞的空竹，让
头脑作出正确的判断，这样不仅全
身关节都得到了不同程度的运动，
视力、四肢的协调能力、大脑的灵
敏度等也都得到了锻炼。此外，抖
空竹还能够启迪人们的想象力和创
造力，使人充满成就感。

above the clouds", etc. The most breath-taking trick is "ant climbing up the tree" which takes two persons to complete: the first person would tie one end of a long string to a branch and hold the other end of the string in his hand; the second person spins the yo-yo and then abruptly tosses the yo-yo toward the long string; the first person then pulls the rope with great force, making the yo-yo soar 50 to 60 meters above the ground. When the yo-yo falls down, the second person who spun the yo-yo would catch and place it steadily on the rope. Anyone who first gets acquainted with this performance will be tremendously impressed and applauded for it.

Though playing a Chinese yo-yo seems to be a very simple exercise for the upper limbs, it actually involves the whole body. When people spin a Chinese yo-yo, they need to be highly concentrated. While playing different tricks, they should always keep their eyes on the yo-yo spinning up and down, so as to make timely decisions with their brains. Consequently, joints of the whole body will be exercised to different degrees, the coordination between the eyes and the limbs enhanced, and agility of the brain improved. Apart

北京长椿街的空竹雕塑
The sculpture of a Chinese yo-yo in the Changchunjie Street, Beijing

抖空竹是深受人们喜爱的集娱乐性、健身性、技巧性、表演性于一体的体育运动，男女老少皆宜，且不受时间、场地的限制。2006年5月20日，抖空竹经国务院批准列入第一批《国家级非物质文化遗产名录》。

from this, playing Chinese yo-yo is inspiring, making people creative and bringing them a sense of achievement.

Playing Chinese yo-yo is a very popular sport among the Chinese, for it's not only entertaining and healthy, but also requires performing skills. This sport, not restricted by time and location, is good for all people, men and women, young and old. It was listed in the first batch on the National Intangible Cultural Heritage List by the State Council on May 20, 2006.

三言两语 A FEW REMARKS

退休之后我经常去公园遛弯儿，慢慢就接触了空竹。开始还不好意思练，怕抖不好丢面子，后来发现并不难，很容易就学会了，再说锻炼身体也没什么可丢人的。玩儿到第三个年头时，胃也不痛了，腰也不酸了，就连失眠的毛病也无影无踪了。走在街上，还有人问我看起来这么年轻，有什么保健秘方呢！

[中国] 郭永健，男，退休工人

现在孩子们的锻炼主要就是做操、跳绳、下棋，亟待补充其他体育项目。抖空竹不但可以强身健体，也具有很好的观赏性，更重要的是它传承了我们的民族文化，孩子们学习抖空竹能真正学到有我们民族特色的东西。

[中国] 柯瑞，女，小学校长

在小伙伴当中，说起抖空竹，大家都夸我抖得好。空竹是一个非常好的健身项目，它既可以锻炼人的四肢，又可以锻炼人的眼力和平衡能力。

After retirement I often took a walk in the park and there I got acquainted with Chinese yo-yo. In the beginning I was too shy to play it, not willing to humiliate myself by playing badly. But later I realized that it was not as difficult as it seems and that there was no humiliation in doing exercises. Three years of playing Chinese yo-yo cured me of stomachaches, backaches and insomnia. When my friends see me on the street, they often ask me what makes me look younger than my age.

[China] Guo Yongjian, male, retired worker

At present children exercise mainly through broadcast gymnastics, rope skipping and playing chess. Many more sports are needed. Playing Chinese yo-yo is an ideal one, not only good for health, but also pleasant to the eyes. More importantly, it's part of our traditional culture through which children can truly grasp the uniqueness of our nation.

[China] Ke Rui, female, primary school headmaster

When it comes to playing Chinese yo-yo, all my friends praise me for my playing it well. It is a very good way to keep fit, for it not only strengthens our legs and arms, but also trains our eyesight and ability to keep balance. Playing Chinese yo-yo is a unique

抖空竹还是我们统一路小学四年级的特色课外活动，我已经在学校认真学习过三个多月了，越来越感兴趣，以后我会抖得更好。

[中国]武子皓，男，小学生

extracurricular activity in my school, Tongyilu Primary School. I have learned it attentively at school for over three months and I am becoming more and more interested. I think I will play better in the future.

[China] Wu Zihao, male, primary school student

小链接 ADDITIONAL INFORMATION

《俏花旦——集体空竹》是国际杂技舞台同类节目中最具有代表性、最具知名度的节目之一。演员多穿着具有京剧艺术元素的服饰进行表演，技巧的设计也很新颖巧妙，既有高难动作，又不失轻松愉快的风格。"跑

《俏花旦——集体空竹》表演
A team performance of Chinese yo-yo, Pretty Prima Donna

肩二节接空竹"、"四层叠罗汉尖子后翻落地二节接空竹"、"三点翻接空竹"、"三小翻接空竹"等技巧组合为当今杂技舞台所罕见。该节目曾于 2005 年获得第 26 届法国明日国际杂技节最高奖——法兰西共和国总统奖。

Pretty Prima Donna, a team performance of Chinese yo-yo, is one of the most representative and well-known acrobatic performances of its liking on the international arena. Performers usually dress in clothes with artistic elements of Peking Opera. Albeit the novel and ingenious techniques and breath-taking tricks in the performance, the ambience is nevertheless amusing and relaxing. The combination of various staggering tricks such as "catching the Chinese yo-yo after spinning it around the shoulder twice" and "catching the yo-yo after backwards somersaults on a four-man pyramid", "catching the yo-yo after three somersaults" and "catching the yo-yo after three minor somersaults" is rarely seen in acrobatic performances today. The performance won the French President Award, the highest award at the 26th Festival Mondial du Cirque De Demain (French Tomorrow International Acrobatics Festival) in 2005.

武术—拳术
Martial Arts – Chinese Boxing

导入 INTRODUCTION

电影《少林寺》宣传海报
Poster of the movie Shaolin Temple

《少林寺》是一部在武侠电影史上具有划时代意义的作品，影片把十三棍僧救唐王的历史传奇与一个为报父仇、出家学武的惊险故事融合在一起，通过李连杰等武术运动员朴素真实的表演，让观众欣赏到了中国武术的真功夫与真精神。《少林寺》于 1982 年公映，在当年一毛钱一张电影票的时代创下了上亿的票房。

Shaolin Temple is an epoch-making production in the history of martial arts movies. It integrates the historical romance of the 13 kungfu monks saving the King of Tang with an adventure of a person learning martial arts to avenge his father. Through the plain and authentic performance of Jet Li and other martial arts players, this movie successfully conveys the true strength and spirit of Chinese martial arts. *Shaolin Temple*, screened in 1982, set a box-office record of more than one hundred million seats sold in a time when a film ticket costed only ten cents.

武术是几千年来中国人强身健体、自卫御敌的方法，也是中国传统的体育项目。武术包括拳术和器械术，拳术是徒手技法的总称，器械术则指手中有武器的武术。

俗话说："天下功夫出少林。"

For thousands of years, martial art has not only been a way for Chinese people to strengthen their bodies and defend themselves, it is also a traditional Chinese sport. It includes Chinese boxing and weapon operations, the former is the general name for bare-handed skills and the latter is also referred to as armed martial arts.

少林寺武僧演练传统少林拳
A Shaolin kungfu monk exercising with traditional Shaolin boxing

As the saying goes "martial arts all over China originated in Shaolin Temple." In the Central Plains of China, Shaolin martial art is the most widespread and diverse school of martial arts that enjoys the longest history standing. It is named after Shaolin Temple in the Song Mountain area of Henan Province. With its unique style, vigorous and forceful movements as well as expertise in striking, Shaolin boxing stands apart from other forms of martial arts.

少林武术是中原武术中范围最广、历史最长、种类最多的武术门派，因源于河南嵩山少林寺而得名。少林拳风格独特，动作刚健有力，擅长技击，在武术界中独树一帜。

Shaolin boxing requires its learners to master the basics, namely standing on poles. Including those for horse-riding stance, chair-shaped, and T-shaped poles, etc. At the same time watching, listening, grabbing, pulling, pushing, lifting and kicking practices are also executed. "Punching in a straight line" is the most distinctive character of Shaolin boxing. To achieve this principle, eight essentials are required, namely, raising, descending, advancing, retreating, reversing, flanking, withholding, and releasing. Being straightforward with plain actions, the series of skills are performed following the same imaginary line which is clearly evidenced by the deep footprints left during practices in the Thousand Buddha Hall of the Shaolin Temple.

少林拳首先要求练好基本功，即站桩。桩有马步桩、椅子桩、丁字桩等，同时也练视、听、抓、拉、推、举、踢等。"拳打一条线"是少林拳最鲜明的特点，法有八要，即起、落、进、退、反、侧、收、纵。套路直来直往，动作朴实，几种套路演练均在一条线上，现在少林寺千佛殿上练拳留下的脚窝就是明证。

Compared with the more aggressive weapon operation, boxing puts much more emphasis on fitness building and self-defense. There

如果说器械术更多的带有攻击性的话，那么拳术则更多的是出于健身、防御的目的。有一套拳术叫"五禽戏"，由东汉医学家华佗创制，其招式模仿了虎、鹿、熊、猿、鹤五种动物的动作，健身效果为历代养生学家所称赞。

中国武术讲究"内练精气神，外练筋骨皮"，即把内在精神与外部动作紧密结合起来。精神委顿、劲力不足的人在练拳的时候必是掌无力、眼无神、身不灵、步不稳；反之，练拳不讲究手眼身法步，所谓外形不合规矩，那么精神、气息、力量、功夫也难以练成。当然，"醉拳"是个例外。这种拳打起来很像醉汉酒后摇摇摆摆、跌跌撞撞的样子，但实际上是形醉意不醉，意醉心不醉。其招法——摔打、推拿、跌扑、

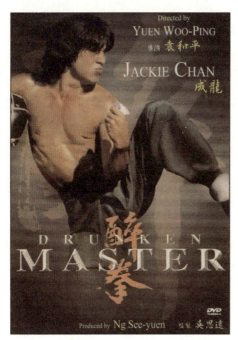

成龙主演的《醉拳》（1978年香港思远影业公司出品）
The hero Jackie Chan in the movie Drunken Master (produced by Seasonal Film Corporation of Hong Kong in 1978)

is a set of boxing skills called the "five-animal exercise" which was created by a medical scientist named Hua Tuo in the Eastern Han Dynasty. The exercise imitates actions of

"五禽戏"雕塑
Sculpture of five-animal exercise

five kinds of animals: tigers, deers, bears, apes, and cranes; its fitness-building effect has always received compliments from generations of health preservation scientists.

Chinese martial arts seek the cultivation of internal spirit and external strength which means a close connection of inner spirit and external movements. People who have a poor mental status and lack physical strengths are destined to encounter powerless palms, dull eyes, clumsy body and unstable legs. On the contrary, if the requirements on hands, eyes, body and steps are not met (failure of observing the rules), it would be difficult to master such elements as spirit, breath, strength and technique. Nevertheless, drunken boxing is an exception. Performance of this kind of boxing looks like a drunken man's waddling and blundering. However, the performer is only drunken in appearance but not in mind

翻滚、窜蹦、跳跃，既充满了形体艺术的美感，又不失技击实用的特点。

中国武术作为一种文化形式，在长期的历史演变中深受中国古代哲学、医学、美学等方面的影响，如太极拳即接受了道家《易经》的思想。其动作特点是：中正安舒、轻灵圆活、松柔慢匀、开合有序、刚柔相济，如行云流水般连绵不断。这种运动既自然又高雅，有音乐的韵律、哲学的内涵、美术的造型、诗歌的意境，可以全面促进人的身心健康。

太极拳
Taijiquan

在世界上，太极拳也受到了各国人民的欢迎。据不完全统计，仅美国就已有30多种太极拳书籍出版，许多国家还成立了太极拳协会等团体，积极与中国进行交流活动。

or consciousness. The skills which include beating, pushing and pulling, tumbling, rolling, leaping and jumping, and contains not only the aesthetic sense of physical art but also the practicality of striking techniques.

Chinese martial arts, as a cultural form, are deeply influenced by ancient Chinese philosophy, medical science and aesthetics in the long process of historical development. For instance, *taijiquan* (tai chi) embraces thoughts from the Taoist classic *The Book of Changes*. *Taijiquan* has the following features: posing steadily and comfortably, circulating with lightness, stretching and closing with regularity, balancing force and tenderness, moving continuously as floating clouds and flowing water. This kind of sport is both natural and elegant, which possesses the melody of music, philosophical meaning, aesthetic shapes and the imagination of poetry, altogether enhancing people's physical and emotional health from all aspects.

Taijiquan is welcomed by people in every country of the world. According to incomplete statistics, America alone has published more than thirty kinds of books concerning *taijiquan*. Besides, many countries have set up communities such as *taijiquan* associations to promote related communication with China.

三言两语 A FEW REMARKS

我在美国教汉语，我们班上男孩子多，提起武术那可不得了，大家都很兴奋，一下子就能把课堂气氛带得很high。他们不仅知道"武术"这个名词，就是说起李小龙、李连杰、成龙这些人和他们的事儿都是如数家珍，没有一个不知道的。我想，这就是中国武术的魅力吧！

[中国]周菲菲，女，汉语教师

我在英国有自己的产业，也有公司，用中国话来说，我是个吃穿不愁的家伙。办武术学校是因为我太喜欢武术了，中国武术尤其让我着迷，能在山清水秀的环境中练武，是我们习武者最大的快乐！

[英国]斯考特，男，武术学校校长

I teach Chinese in America. There are more boys in my class, so at the time of referring to Chinese martial arts, students are so excited that the atmosphere becomes very hot. Not only do each and every one of them know the phrase "Chinese martial arts", they also know a great deal about such figures such as Bruce Lee, Jet Li and Jackie Chan. Maybe, I guess, this is the charm of Chinese martial arts!

[China] Zhou Feifei, female, Chinese teacher

I have my own property and company in Britain, in other words, I don't have to worry about food and clothing. I'm running a martial arts school out of sheer love. Chinese martial arts cast a spell on me. Nothing can be happier than practicing martial arts in an environment surrounded by green mountains and clean water!

[Britain] Scott, male, martial arts school headmaster

小链接 ADDITIONAL INFORMATION

跆拳道是韩国武术，由品势、对抗、击破等部分组成。跆拳道具有较高的强身健体、防御自卫的实用价值，并能培养坚忍不拔的意志。跆(TAE)意为以脚踢、摔撞，拳(KWON)即以拳头打击，道(DO)是一种艺术方法。跆拳道有着深厚的文化内涵，以"始于礼，终于礼"的武道精神为基础。目前跆拳道是奥运会比赛项目，国际上有世界跆拳道联盟（WTF）和国际跆拳道联盟（ITF）两大组织，民间的跆拳道组织不可胜数。

跆拳道
Taekwondo

Taekwondo is a kind of Korean martial art comprising gesture holding, confrontation and conquering. It has a practical value of building up the body and defending oneself; besides it can also develop people's perseverance. "Tae" means kicking and also for bumping; "kwon" means punching with fists; and "do" is a method of art. Taekwondo embodies profound cultural connotations and is based on the spirit of martial arts described as starting and ending with courtesy. Nowadays, taekwondo has become one of the sport events in the Olympic Games. There are two international taekwondo organizations, namely, the World Taekwondo Federation (WTF) and the International Taekwondo Federation (ITF); besides there are still numerous non-governmental taekwondo organizations in the world.